TRAVELLERS

TANZANIA &
ZANZIBAR

By
DAVID WATS

Written and updated by David Watson

Original photography by David Watson

Editing and page layout by Cambridge Publishing Management Ltd,
Unit 2, Burr Elm Court, Caldecote CB23 7NU

Series Editor: Karen Beaulah

Published by Thomas Cook Publishing
A division of Thomas Cook Tour Operations Limited
Company Registration No. 1450464 England

PO Box 227, The Thomas Cook Business Park,
Coningsby Road, Peterborough PE3 8SB, United Kingdom
E-mail: books@thomascook.com
www.thomascookpublishing.com

ISBN: 978-1-84157-795-1

Text © 2007 Thomas Cook Publishing
Maps © 2007 Thomas Cook Publishing
First edition © 2005 Thomas Cook Publishing
Second edition © 2007 Thomas Cook Publishing

Project Editor: Rebecca Snelling
Production/DTP Editor: Steven Collins

Printed and bound in Italy by: Printer Trento.

Front cover credits: © Breck P Kent/Photolibrary; © Ariadne Van
Zandbergen/Photolibrary; © Ariadne Van Zandbergen/Photolibrary
Back cover credits: © Carlos Navajas/Getty Images; © blickwinkel/Alamy

Contents

KEY TO MAPS

✈ Airport   ▲ 3840m Mountain

B144 Road number   ♠ Accommodation

⛅ Swamp   ⓘ Information

Introduction

Tanzania is a country of superlatives: the highest, the longest and the deepest. Kilimanjaro is the highest and the most massive free-standing mountain on the planet. The eastern and western arms of the Great Rift Valley are like two enormous gashes, running the length of the country, and surrounded by spectacular volcanic scenery. Ngorongoro is the world's largest complete crater and, as the location of Ngorongoro National Park, is described by many as the eighth Wonder of the World.

Lake Tanganyika is, as yet, way off most tourist trails, but is the longest body of fresh water on the planet, is the second deepest, and is host to more endemic species than almost anywhere else – testimony to the length of its existence. Where else on Earth is it possible to view two million wildebeest and zebra on their relentless annual migration but in the Serengeti National Park? This is surely one of the most amazing wildlife spectacles available. Further south in the Selous Game Reserve, we have the largest game reserve in Africa, and one of the biggest on Earth. Tanzania is truly a land of superlatives.

Culturally too the country is amazing. Oldupai (formerly Olduvai), on the edge of Serengeti is described as one of the Cradles of Civilisation, and throughout the northern part of the

Dust clouds accompany the herds

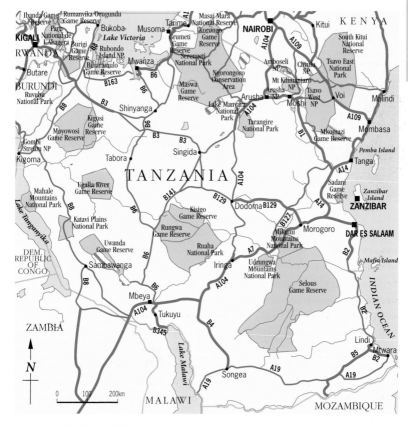

country is the home of the Maasai, probably most famous of all of the tribes of Africa, still dressed in red, herding cattle and enormously proud of their traditions and rituals.

The coast too is the home of the distinctive Swahili Culture, a blend of Bantu African with Arabic, Indian and a smattering of Portuguese and British. This unique combination produced a trading system which was over 1,000 years old even when Vasco da Gama arrived in 1498. One element is the Kiswahili language; another is the distinctive architecture found in the Stone Town of Zanzibar, unique in Africa south of the equator with hundreds of buildings dating from the 19th century and earlier.

However, most people will visit Tanzania for one of two reasons: for the coast and to go on safari. The coral sand beaches of both the mainland and the islands are superb, and are often empty and relatively undeveloped. Diving at sites such as Fundu Lagoon, Mnemba Atoll and Mafia Island is among the best in the world.

Geography and climate

Tanzania lies a few degrees south of the equator and, at 945,090sq km (364,900sq miles), is the biggest country in East Africa, roughly the same size as Egypt or Venezuela, and about twice as big as California. It has a long, coral-fringed coastline that runs along the Indian Ocean, and has land borders with seven other African countries: Kenya, Mozambique, Malawi, Burundi, Zambia, Rwanda and Uganda.

The country has a spectacular range of scenery. The northern two-thirds is high plateau, the southern third is lower, everywhere punctuated by amazing landscape features. Kilimanjaro lies next to the border with Kenya, and is Africa's highest peak. Running north to south through the country are the east and west arms of the Great African Rift Valley, often forming a huge gash in the landscape. Occupying parts of the western valley are the huge lakes of Tanganyika and Nyasa. Lake Tanganyika is the longest freshwater lake, and the second deepest in the world. Between the two arms of the Rift Valley is Lake Victoria, the second-biggest lake in the world.

There are huge volcanic highlands, especially in the north, with the massive crater of Ngorongoro and the still-active Ol Doinyo Lengai as two of its stars. Adjacent to the highlands are the volcanic, ash-covered plains of the Serengeti, possibly the most famous wildlife area in the world. In the south are other, more remote highlands, such as the Kipengere Range and the Livingstone Mountains. Many areas are isolated and undeveloped, especially in the south and centre, giving rise to the formation of some of Africa's largest game reserves such as Selous and Rungwa.

There is a narrow coastal plain, and there are numerous islands, the biggest of which are Zanzibar, Pemba and Mafia. The coast is mainly fringed by a coral reef, before the seabed

The great Ruaha River

plunges down into the depths of the Indian Ocean.

Rufiji, the biggest river, flows through Selous Game Reserve and forms a large but inaccessible delta, south of Dar es Salaam.

Other rivers include the Ruvuma, flowing along the border with Mozambique, the Pangani, which flows from Kilimanjaro, and the Lukuledi. Often, as a result of rivers bringing silt into the sea, there is a break in the coral reef, and one finds areas of the salt-tolerating mangroves, especially in deltas and estuaries.

The climate

The climate is basically tropical, though this is modified by altitude. So the daytime temperature is usually about 30°C (86°F) on the coast, about 20°C (68°F) on the rim of Ngorongoro Crater and freezing at 5,000m (16,400ft) on Kilimanjaro. Night temperatures have a similar range, ending up warm and muggy at the coast, quite cool most places inland and cold in the mountains.

Tanzania has two periods of rainfall which occur just after the two equinoxes, though the further south, away from the equator, as one can see from the Mbeya climate statistics, it is more likely there will be only one longer rainy period. Also, it is a reasonable rule of thumb that mountains will receive more rain than lowlands.

Over much of the country, the long rains are generally from March to May, and the short rains from October to December. However, except in exceptional times, as in the 1998 El Nino, it rarely rains continuously. Undoubtedly the rains make travel difficult, but it is still possible to have a mainly sunny and warm holiday at the beach, even during the rainy periods. Probably the most obvious problem for the visitor from a temperate country is the high level of humidity sometimes found at the coast.

Coconut plantation

Geography and climate

Climate statistics

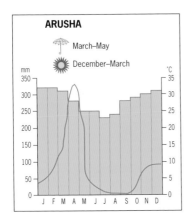

ARUSHA
March–May
December–March

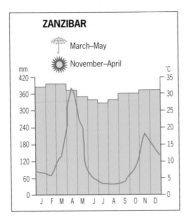

ZANZIBAR
March–May
November–April

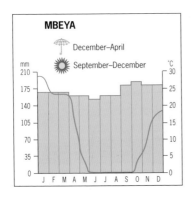

MBEYA
December–April
September–December

The plants

The pattern of Tanzania's plants mainly reflects variations in rainfall, but in the mountains temperature decrease also becomes very important.

Along the coast, the original forest is almost all gone. Mangroves occur where rivers reach the sea, as with the Amboni at Tanga, and in most places there are coconut palms.

In much of the interior, you'll find a variety of tropical savannah, with varying amounts of woodlands. Much is miombo, giving way to different forms of acacia as one moves north. In most of the central part of the country, but also on the coast, one sees giant baobab trees, with their enormous trunks giving them huge water-storage facility. Further west, beyond Ngorongoro are the volcanic ash-covered grassland plains of Serengeti.

Rivers and watercourses are testified to by the enormous, Congo-like diversity of plants, following the valleys. In dry areas, with seasonal watercourses, it is still common to find

Rubondo Island jungle

crotons and euclea bushes following the path of water underground.

Mountains create a dramatic vegetational sequence. Kilimanjaro, especially, allows a bio-transect equivalent to travelling from the equator to the poles as one makes the ascent. At the bottom, there is tropical savannah, with acacia trees, but soon the climber enters montane and bamboo forest. Beyond is a zone of strange, giant plants, with tree heathers and huge alpines such as giant lobelia. Higher still, the mountain is covered in a sort of moorland, and then tundra, with plants frozen every night. Eventually there are permanent snow and glaciers, with conditions the same as at the poles.

In the towns, you can see the influence of the waves of immigrant plant-life over the centuries. Exotics such as jacaranda, hibiscus and bougainvillea are common.

The fauna

Tanzania is quite simply one of the most amazing locations on Earth to view tropical wildlife. Serengeti has the world's most thrilling annual migrations; Tarangire is the best place in Africa to view elephants; the Rufiji River has the highest densities of crocodiles.

On the coast and around the islands there are some of the best coral reefs you can find anywhere, with over 200 species of coral and over 400 species of fish in a number of locations.

There are many superb birdwatching locations, and the mountain rainforests, such as the Usambaras, are simply brilliant for butterflies.

A lilac-breasted roller in flight

History

Prehistory

3.6 million years ago	Human-like footprints made in Laotoli mud, discovered by Mary Leakey in 1976.
2 million years ago	*Australopithecus boisei* is living on the site of present-day Oldupai (formerly Olduvai) Gorge.
10,000 years ago	Modern bushmen live in Tanzania.
500–1,000 years ago	Arrival of the first Cushites from the north, probably from Ethiopia.

The Arabs

1st and 2nd centuries AD	Trading pattern in the Indian Ocean already well established, and mentioned by Ptolemy in AD 150.
AD **200–300**	First Bantu-speakers begin to arrive in East Africa from the west.
Late 700s	Arrival of Islam with Arab traders.
1107	Building of oldest mosque in Tanzania.

1300–1500	Establishment of the great trading cities of the coast of East Africa – places like Kilwa, Mombasa and Lamu.

The Portuguese

1498	Vasco da Gama arrives off the coast of East Africa only six years after Columbus discovers America.
1500s and 1600s	Ruled by Portugal.
1503	Portugal captures Unguja Island.
1506	Portugal captures Pemba.
1560	Portuguese build small settlement on west coast of Unguja, eventually to become Zanzibar town.

The Omanis

1650	The Portuguese are overthrown in Zanzibar.
1668	Omanis have control over the coast of East Africa except

for Mombasa and Zanzibar (Stone Town).

1698   200 years after they arrive, the Portuguese are eventually driven out for good.

1700–1800   Steady increase in slavery under Omanis.

Late 1700s   Maasai begin to arrive from Nile Valley in southern Sudan.

1822   Sultan Said signs anti-slavery treaty with Britain, limiting the transport of slaves within the Indian Ocean.

1827   Arrival of Sultan Said in Zanzibar. First clove plantation established in Zanzibar; massive increase in demand for slaves.

1840   Omani capital moves from Muscat to Zanzibar.

Marahubi Palace

By 1840	40,000 slaves a year now involved in slave trading.
1840s	Ngoni people arrive in southern Tanzania from the south.
1840–70	Europeans 'discover' the great lakes of East Africa.
1871	The year when Stanley famously said, 'Dr Livingstone, I presume.'
1873	Slave trading eventually abolished.
1890	Britain and Germany agree on the carve-up of East Africa. Tanganyika becomes a German colony.
1914–18	First World War.
1918	Germany surrenders to the British and their allies.
1919	Tanganyika mandated to Britain in Treaty of Versailles.
1929	The Tanganyika African Association is founded – the effective beginning of independence.
1947	Tanganyika becomes 'trustee territory' under the United Nations.
1954	Tanganyika African National Union is formed.

Since independence

December 1961	Full independence from Britain; Julius Nyerere becomes prime minister.
December 1962	Tanganyika becomes a republic; Julius Nyerere becomes first president.
December 1963	Zanzibar gains independence.

Maasai Boy near Mount Lemakarot

A colonial legacy – cricket still survives in Dar es Salaam

January 1964	Revolt deposes the Sultan of Zanzibar, who is forced to flee.
April 1964	Tanzania created by the union of Tanganyika and Zanzibar.
1967	Arusha Declaration sets up *Ujamaa*, the collectivisation of villages using a socialist model, which eventually fails.
1979	Tanzanian army topples Ugandan dictator Idi Amin.
1985	Julius Nyerere resigns and hands over power peacefully to President Ali Hassan Mwinyi.
1995	Benjamin Mkapa becomes president and Tanzania changes political direction, from socialism to capitalism. A multi-party democracy is created. Tanzania comes in from the political cold.
1998	Al-Qaeda bombs US embassies in Nairobi and Dar es Salaam. Over 300 killed.
1999	Following political reforms, Tanzania becomes one of the first countries in the world to achieve major debt relief with the granting of Highly Indebted Country Status.
2001	Mkapa returns to power. He is accused of electoral fraud, but remains president.
2004	Tanzania hosts International Criminal Tribunal for Rwanda in Arusha.
2005	Mkapa ia returned for a further term in the October elections.
2010	Next scheduled presidential election.

Dr David Livingstone

David Livingstone as a young man

Dr David Livingstone is probably the most famous of the European explorers and missionaries from the 19th century. He was born in 1813 in the Scottish town of Blantyre, south of Glasgow. He completed his medical training and became an ordained minister. Livingstone had heard of the work of the Scottish missionary Robert Moffat, and was so inspired by his example that he set out for southern Africa as a missionary in 1841. In 1849 he became the first European to cross the Kalahari Desert and from 1852 to 1856 followed the Zambezi River from its source to its mouth, en route becoming the first European to see the falls which he named 'Victoria' after his queen.

He married Robert Moffat's daughter, Mary, and they had six children. His family often travelled with him into the wilderness, but they were frequently separated for lengthy periods, the longest, in the 1850s, for five years. Mary died in 1862 from an African fever (presumably malaria).

Livingstone spent his life engaged in a wide range of activities: missionary, doctor, explorer, scientist and anti-slave activist. It was at a village on the Lualaba River that Livingstone first witnessed slave traders engaged in the slaughter of villagers, and as a result of his fury, the UK government began the pressurising of the Sultan of Zanzibar to abolish slave trading. This eventually ended in the year of Livingstone's death, in 1873.

Livingstone set out on his most famous journey in 1865, exploring the watershed of central Africa and searching for the source of the Nile, a peculiarly British preoccupation in the 19th century. Nothing was heard of him for several years and a search expedition was mounted and led by fellow explorer Henry Morton Stanley. The two eventually met in 1871 at Ujiji on the shores of Lake Tanganyika, and Stanley was reported to have uttered the immortal words, 'Dr Livingstone, I presume.'

Livingstone's navigational instruments

Livingstone was very weak and malnourished, but instead of returning to the coast, he accepted the supplies Stanley had brought, and continued on his journey, relentlessly searching for the source of the Nile, which he never found. He eventually died, suffering from dysentery and worn out from his travels. His loyal African assistants buried his heart, and then, amazingly, carried his dried and preserved body over 1,500km (932 miles) to Nairobi. He was then transported to England where he was buried in London's Westminster Abbey, normally the final resting place in Britain for kings and queens. Stanley's apt words at the funeral were, 'Livingstone's body is buried here, but his heart lies in Africa.' The famous nurse Florence Nightingale said, 'God has taken away the greatest man of his generation.'

Livingstone is remembered for a number of things, but probably mainly as the greatest southern African explorer, revealing the great rivers and lakes in the formerly 'dark continent' to the rest of the world. Also, his effect as a catalyst in achieving the end of slave trading must not be underestimated.

David Livingstone, later in life, missionary and explorer

Politics

When the Portuguese explorer Vasco da Gama arrived at Kilwa in 1498, he found a series of successful trading states under the control of Shirazi rulers from the Persian Gulf. From then until 1698, the Portuguese ruled, to be followed by the Omanis, who ultimately had their capital in Zanzibar. At the end of the 19th century, Tanganyika became a German colony. From 1916 until final independence, it was ruled by the British.

After independence

Tanganyika became an independent country in December 1961. More than 40 years later, perhaps its greatest achievement is that it has not suffered from the catastrophic effects of tribalism, which have beset most of its neighbours. One of the reasons for this is undoubtedly the unifying effect of the national language, Swahili, taught in schools throughout the country.

Photograph of portrait of Julius Nyerere from National Museum

Soon after independence, it became clear that new leader Julius Nyerere would lean well to the left of the political spectrum, and away from the capitalistic West.

Zanzibar gained its independence two years later, in December 1963, but trouble soon followed. In the elections, the Afro-Shirazi party had received most of the popular vote, but did not get most of the seats; control of government went to the mainly Arab Zanzibar National Party. Within a month, in a violent, popular uprising, the Sultan was deposed and about 12,000 Arabs were killed; the rest fled. In April 1964, an Act of Union joined together Tanganyika and Zanzibar, and Tanzania was created. The country was now a republic, with Nyerere as president and Karume, leader in Zanzibar, as vice-president.

During this time, Julius Nyerere was becoming increasingly disenchanted with his former colonial masters. When

Rhodesia's Ian Smith made an illegal declaration of independence, Nyerere felt that Britain had meekly accepted this, and should have been much more active in its opposition. He broke off diplomatic relations with Britain, and Tanzania began a rapid drift towards socialism and specifically the Republic of China, which was to build and finance the railway from Tanzania to Zambia during the early 1970s.

Ujamaa

The cornerstone, and ultimate reason for the failure of Nyerere's policies for the country, was *Ujamaa* ('familyhood' or togetherness). Under this policy, the rural population of Tanzania would abandon their age-old practice of living in scattered villages, and move to collectives, where production of food would be done communally, and where there would be schools, clinics, clean water and electricity. Socially it was an initial success, but economically, and from the point of view of food production, it was a disaster.

The people refused to move, and after three years only four per cent of the population were in *Ujamaa* villages. Eventually, coercion was the only way; the farmers were forced to move and, by 1977, 80 per cent were living in collective villages. Though Tanzania's literacy rates were among the highest in Africa and there was primary health care for all, agricultural output dropped, water supplies were often inadequate and Tanzania slipped further into rural poverty. Even today, about half of the population is below the internationally accepted poverty line. *Ujamaa* had failed, and Nyerere was disillusioned.

Aga Khan Hospital, one of the medical facilities in Dar es Salaam

African house in the Village Museum

International politics

Meanwhile, Nyerere was busy acting as international broker throughout Africa, at the expense of his own country, some said at the time. He encouraged a variety of freedom fighters, from Rhodesia (now Zimbabwe), Angola and Mozambique, and even set up training camps in Tanzania.

In 1977, the East African Community Free Trade Zone – made up of a capitalist Kenya, a left-wing Tanzania and a Ugandan dictatorship – not surprisingly collapsed. The border with Kenya was closed, and remained so for the next five years.

In 1979, much to the applause of the rest of the world, a poorly trained Tanzanian force invaded Uganda and removed dictator Idi Amin, who fled to Libya. However, poverty-stricken Tanzania was left to foot the $500 million bill, for being both East Africa's conscience and policeman.

During the late 1970s and 1980s, as the failure of *Ujama* was becoming evident to everyone, the major governments of the world became increasingly alienated, sources of funding dried up and the country slid further and further into poverty.

Socialism abandoned – back to capitalism

In 1985, Julius Nyerere resigned as president in the first voluntary handover of power in independent Africa. The new president was Ali Hassan Mwinyi. The period since then has seen the abandonment of many socialist principles, including *Ujama* and a move towards private enterprise. Over the period, Tanzania has begun to see annual economic growth of about four per cent.

Allied to this, and as part of changes demanded by the IMF and the World Bank as the price for Tanzania coming back under their umbrella, the one-party state has been replaced once more by multi-party politics, with several political parties contesting elections, and by an attack on corruption. However, the path has not been smooth, with allegations of electoral fraud, especially in Zanzibar, being substantiated by impartial observers, both in 1995 and again in 2000.

Perhaps the biggest step forward has been in the area of international debt, the millstone which cripples so many African countries.

Tanzania became one of the first countries in the world to be given the status of Highly Indebted Poor Country (HIPC), and so qualified for massive debt relief.

The future

Tanzania remains one of the world's 25 poorest countries. The GNP per capita is only $250 a year, and 30 per cent of the people still live in abject poverty. It remains one of the most agriculturally dependent countries in the world, with only 15 per cent of the people being classified as 'urban'.

But things are improving. To translate its effect to grass roots, the economy is growing spectacularly at over 3 per cent a year. Tanzania is now back in the world fold, where it has been granted debt relief, and is receiving aid and increasing international investment. What is now required is for the effects of growth and improvements in infrastructure and other reforms to be felt in the lives of the people.

Sunni Muslim School, Stone Town

Culture

Culture is an important and lively element in Tanzania's life. In the past, the Swahili culture of the East African coast produced its own art forms, especially in its distinctive architecture. Today, the most important artistic areas by far are the performing arts of music and dance, though there is a tourist-driven vigour and ready market for painting and sculpture.

Architecture

The Stone Town of Zanzibar exhibits the best range of Swahili architecture in the world, albeit much of it in a crumbling condition. It mainly stems from the 19th century when the influence of Oman was at its height.

The classical Swahili house has, first and foremost, a huge and ornately carved doorway. Tradition dictated that the doorway was the first part of the house to be built. Over 500 of these doors still exist in the Stone Town. Inside there is a courtyard and a verandah. Often the houses were semi-fortified, with castellated walls. Groups of houses were built in blocks called *mitaa*, each *mitaa* with its own mosque, coffee shop etc.

Tingatinga

Tingatinga is the most important modern art form to have developed in Tanzania. It was started by Edward Saidi Tingatinga, who was born at Namonchelia, in southern Tanzania, in 1932. He did not begin painting until 1968, and died soon after at the age of 40, when he was shot by police during a car chase. However, in his short artistic life he developed a simple, bold and colourful style of painting. It is highly decorative, but childlike, and uses bright, high-gloss colours in oils.

Tingatinga has about 50 'students' who continue his style, mainly for the tourist trade.

Makonde

For many, the carvings of the Makonde tribe from southern Tanzania and

Tingatinga paintings

northern Mozambique are by far the most important art form to come out of the whole of East Africa. The carvings usually follow one of three forms, daily life, the family or togetherness, and a grotesque form called *shetani* (the devil), which is based on Makonde spirits. Makonde carvers are now mainly based in Dar es Salaam and Arusha.

The art of women

Women have a distinctive role in art in Tanzania, traditionally producing the crafts, weaving, pottery etc.

At Bagamoyo Living Art Centre a group of women is involved in weaving, tie-dye, batik and pottery.

In various Usambara villages, such as Kileti, there are about 30 women potters who are responsible for the entire process, from collecting clay, to making and firing the pots.

Music and dance

Music and dancing are undoubtedly the most vibrant of all the art forms in

President Mkapa sculpture, Village Museum

Tanzania. Probably it is the only major art form not driven by tourism. It is the music and dance of the people. Though there are modern forms driven by radio and modern recording, traditional music and dance have not been lost. The word *ngoma*, 'dance', is also the Swahili word for 'drum', illustrating the importance of rhythm in traditional dancing. Dancing and singing had many forms, including communicating with ancestors. As well as drums, there are many other traditional instruments, such as *marimba* and *kayamba*.

There is a very popular modern form of dancing called *mchirku*, using a combination of modern instruments and drums. Because of the frequently undisguised sexual nature of the songs, the form has been sometimes banned in the past. Today it is presented as the 'Tanzanian Sound'.

Singing and dancing are found in many locations throughout all Tanzanian towns and cities.

National Museum, Dar es Salaam

The Makonde carvers

There is a general belief that Makonde carving represents the greatest and least inhibited art form that East Africa has to offer the world.

Who are the Makonde?

The Makonde are one of five major tribes who migrated north from the Makonde Plateau of Mozambique into the southern highlands of Tanzania. They were relatively unknown until the beginning of the 20th century, but lived in carving communities practising and developing their art form. In the 1950s the first Makonde workshop was set up in Dar es Salaam and 'Makonde' became known to the world.

Their legend is that there was a man, the first man on Earth. He carved a wooden figure, which came to life and became his wife. Their first two children died, and it was only when they moved to the forest in the mountains that they had their third child, who survived.

The mother is the central figure in Makonde society and in Makonde carvings.

What sorts of carvings are there?

In general, Makonde carvings are of figurines or often groups of figures.

There appear to be three main themes or genres. They are:

- *Binadamu*: people carrying out their daily and normal work, doing things like carrying water or hoeing.
- *Ujamaa*: people doing things together. Often these figures are carved in an intricate and entwined form. Frequently there is a central mother figure, with children clinging to her.
- *Shetani*: literally means 'the devil' (Satan). Spiritual figures depicting variously ancestors, spirits, sorcerers etc.

Carvings on display in Dar es Salaam

Additionally some also identify a fourth form that is more abstract, and which is called *mausinga*.

The most important theme in Makonde art is the family, especially the mother figure. It is quite normal for Makonde men to carry a carved female figure for good luck.

The most traditional form of Makonde carving is the mask, representing an ancient spirit. Masks were used in special ceremonies such as initiation, and carved at a place called *mpole*, to which women were forbidden. Masks would be returned there after they were used.

The scale of the works varies. The largest, called 'Tree of Life' carvings, may be 2m (6ft) tall and take many months to complete.

What are they made from?
True Makonde carvings are made from a single block of African blackwood (*Dalbergia melanoxylon*). Though the bark and the sapwood are light coloured, the heartwood is red to black, depending on the age of the tree and the soil quality. Carvers use only this. When the finished carving is polished, the wood shines. The wood is very dense and it is this density of grain that allows the artists to produce such fine detail.

There are modern forms of Makonde art, often produced purely for the tourist market. Modern Makonde figures are said to be 'Modigliani' in style. Well-known Makonde artists include Samaki Likankoa and Dastan Nyedi.

You can see carvers at work in Nyumba ya Sanaa (House of Art), Upanga St, Dar es Salaam. You can also buy carvings from a good selection at Kariakoo and Mwenge markets, in Dar es Salaam.

Makonde carvings being finished

Festivals

In many ways the most important annual celebrations in Tanzania are not of culture, but of wildlife, such as the return in November and December to Serengeti of two million wildebeest and zebra. However, there is one significant time for cultural festivals which take place at the coast and in Zanzibar at the end of June and during July. By far the most important event is the Zanzibar Film Festival.

The Zanzibar Film Festival (Tamasha La Nchi Za Jahazi)

The Zanzibar Film Festival (also known as the Festival of the Dhow Countries) takes place over the two weeks at the end of June and the beginning of July. It is reputedly the biggest annual cultural event in East Africa, and it is among the top ten festivals in Africa.

It started in 1998, and has since grown and diversified rapidly, to include over 100 films, 30 musical and performance events, together with a three-day literary forum, a 'Children's Panorama' and events which promote women in the arts. Out in the villages over 200,000 children celebrate the festival in music and dance in the 'Children's Panorama'.

The main venue for films is the open-air theatre at Omani Fort on the Stone Town waterfront. Other venues are all in the same area, including the Palace Museum, the House of Wonders and the Old Dispensary. Forodhani Gardens, next to the sea, are also much in use.

Many events are free, with others having only a minimal charge. Venues are all conveniently clustered within the western edge of Stone Town, near to and including the House of Wonders. *e-mail: ziff@ziff.or.tz; www.ziff.or.tz*

The Swahili Music Festival (Sauti za Busara)

The Sauti za Busara is a six-day music festival held annually in Zanzibar in mid-February. According to the *Tanzania Daily News*, it is 'the friendliest festival on Planet Earth'. It involves a wide range of music styles,

The Sauti za Busara Music Festival

including traditional *ngoma*, *taarab*, *kidumbak*, *mchiriku* and *musiki wa dansi* (no prizes for translating the last one!). The main venue is the Old Fort in Stone Town.
e-mail: busara@zanlink.com;
www.busaramusic.com

The Mwaka Kongwa Festival

This festival is utterly different and has been going on for about 1,000 years. It lasts only one day and occurs in the last week of July, when the Shirazi New Year is celebrated around Zanzibar. The centre of the celebrations is the village of Makunduchi, in the southeast corner.

There are several annual rituals. One includes mock battles between the men of the north and south of the village, who vent their feelings by beating each other with banana leaves. Any unresolved problems from the old year are supposedly beaten out, and the new year can begin afresh.

Another ritual tradition involves the burning of a specially made palm-leaf hut, which symbolises the destruction of the old spirits of the past year and the creation of a clean place for those of the new.

The celebrations also specifically include hospitality, and it is considered bad luck not to have a visitor staying in your house. The daytime rituals are followed in the evening by feasting, dancing and music.

The Makumbusho Village Museum

This museum hosts different tribal and cultural celebrations most afternoons. There is a small fee for these events.
New Bagamoyo Road, Dar es Salaam.

The Saba Saba International Trade Fair

Saba Saba literally means '7th of the 7th' and is held on Peasants' Day, a national holiday in Tanzania. The venue is the Saba Saba Ground on Kilwa Road in Dar es Salaam. Usually there is a wide range of products on display as well as lots of food and drink.

Festivals

Amphitheatre, Omani Fort

Impressions

'Tanzania' conjures up unique images, not only the setting of the world's greatest safari experiences, such as the Serengeti, but also snow-capped Kilimanjaro, the world's biggest free-standing mountain. Or perhaps the attraction for you is the palm-fringed, coral beaches of the Indian Ocean, and the superb diving of hundreds of reefs. Or maybe you are simply fascinated by a continent which is different, and its wealth of contrasting cultures, such as the Swahilis of the coast and the Maasai of the interior.

When to go?

When you decide to visit Tanzania depends on what you want to do and see there.

Firstly, there is the issue of the weather. There are two rainy seasons which you might want to avoid. The 'long rains' are from March to May, with the 'short rains' from October to December. However, it often rains during the night or for only a short

Maasai *Shuka*

period during the day, and it may not affect your holiday much. Occasionally, though, rains can be torrential and persistent, and seriously affect one's ability to travel, as with the rains during the 1998 El Nino. Further south, the rains tend to be concentrated in only one period, the same time as the Northern Hemisphere winter.

Going at the right time may be especially critical for a safari holiday. For example, wildebeest will be in the southeast Serengeti Plains from December to April, but from July to November most of them are in the Masai Mara in Kenya.

Which areas to visit?

Tanzania is a big country, twice the area of Sweden, for example. Your holiday will therefore be concentrated in one area, or two or three at the most. The classical image of an African holiday is the 'safari' (which in Swahili simply means 'journey'). There are three main safari destinations:

- **The Northern Circuit**, including world-famous locations such as Serengeti and Ngorongoro.
- **The Southern Circuit** – the star attraction of which is Selous, Africa's biggest game reserve, and remote parks like Katavi.
- **The great lakes** of East Africa, and locations such as **Gombe** and **Mahale** on Lake Tanganyika.

Or you may come for the other main attraction, the beach. Tanzania's coasts and islands have all the attractions that allow the brochures to call them 'paradise': white coral sand, palm-fringed beaches and clear azure-blue sea. Your destinations may include:

- **Zanzibar** and **Pemba**.

WALKING AND SECURITY IN ARUSHA

If you choose a 'safari' holiday, Arusha may be your first experience of Africa, so it is a good time to think of personal security. Generally say 'No' to young men who:
- Pester you in the street with offers of safari tours, taxis, hotels, or anything which is a 'special' deal.
- Try to offer you good exchange deals on foreign currency. Above all, never go anywhere with them.

You can avoid much of the danger of mugging by:
- Not conspicuously flaunting your wealth.
- Not walking around at night. Specifically keep out of areas such as Old Moshi Road, and notorious districts such as Sanawari.
- Only taking reputable taxis. Ask at your hotel if it's not clear.
- Keeping your car windows closed in town, and using the air conditioner in your vehicle.

- **Dar es Salaam** and the mainland coast.

The third major reason is to become one of the 20,000 a year who attempt to climb **Kilimanjaro**, the world's biggest free-standing mountain.

How to get around?

If you arrive on an organised tour, you will not have to think about your transport within the country. However, independent travellers will need to decide. How you travel within the country depends on your budget, the amount of time you have and what level of comfort you require.

Most Tanzanians travel by bus and minibus. They are cheap, but often overcrowded, uncomfortable and with an atrocious safety record in comparison with standards in developed countries.

Hire cars are readily available in many locations. Better still, if you are visiting national parks or reserves, you will find that a 4-wheel-drive vehicle

Fully air-conditioned *daladalas*, Zanzibar

will be most suitable. There is a wide range to choose from, but serious safari travellers choose Toyota Land Cruisers or Land Rovers. Best of all, hire from one of the companies that also supply a driver (*see 'Driving' in the Practical Guide on p178*).

In town, you may wish to use the *daladala*, the type of minibus which is the most common transport for most Tanzanians. However, you may prefer to use taxis. They are widely available, but negotiate your fare before you set off.

Or you may choose to fly. There are regular flights from several operators to nearly all tourist destinations, especially safari locations, which receive a large proportion of their clients by air. The views are amazing, but it is expensive.

A culture shock?

Probably the first thing to be aware of is that in visiting Tanzania you are going to one of the world's poorest countries. Half the people are 'poor' by any international measure, and 30 per cent live in conditions which may be

Pavement sellers, Dar es Salaam

described as 'abject poverty'. As an affluent traveller, you do have to decide how you respond in a country of mainly very poor people.

Secondly, most folk on the coast of Tanzania are Muslims. The women are covered, sometimes totally, and one needs to respect Muslim standards. In general, be aware that flimsy and immodest Western dress may be found insulting. Except on the beach, women should cover up, avoiding bare shoulders. It may be acceptable for couples to hold hands, but generally avoid public displays of intimacy.

Photography is offensive to some; it is always better to ask for permission to take photographs, and be prepared to pay.

Greetings

Effusive greetings are important in Tanzania. Most people in East Africa introduce almost every conversation by enquiring about each other's health and wellbeing.

Universally, the word '*Jambo*' is used (meaning 'Hello'). The reply is the

Floating Fish Market, Stone Town

same: '*Jambo*' or '*Sijambo*'. Next might be '*Habari?*' (meaning approximately 'How are you?'). The reply will normally be '*Mzuri*' ('Fine') or '*Mzuri sana*' ('Very well'). After all this, one then moves on to the reason for the conversation. Even if your Swahili is only a few words and phrases, you will be amazed at the cheerful response it brings.

Are there snakes everywhere?

Many people have a snake phobia and may be put off an African holiday because of an unreal expectation that they will be stepping on snakes everywhere. The truth is firstly that you are most unlikely to see even one snake. Secondly, snakes are much more scared of you than you are of them, and thirdly, even folk who live in Tanzania might never see a single snake in a whole year.

You will see lots of harmless lizards, especially the multi-coloured agama and the insect-eating (and therefore very welcome) gecko.

Most snakes are really concerned about hiding from you, and even if there are some around, they disappear long before you can see them. Though they have no ears, they are incredibly sensitive to the vibrations caused by our walking.

The most likely place to see the common snakes of Tanzania will be in a snake park, of which there are many. There you will be able to see common varieties such as African rock python, black-necked spitting cobra, puff adder and black mamba.

Agama lizard, Oldupai

On safari: the northern circuit

To experience the classical safari is the main reason many visitors come to Tanzania, and the majority will head for the northern safari circuit, including Tarangire, Manyara, Ngorongoro and Serengeti. Northern Tanzania represents the epitome of the African safari, with enormous herds of plains animals, and landscapes and habitats of world importance. This is now the world's most important safari destination.

Most tourists will arrive through Arusha, the gateway to the parks and reserves of northern Tanzania.

The majority of the safari tour companies such as the biggest, Leopard Tours, are based in Arusha. However, this is also the place where you can hire your own self-drive Land Rover or Land Cruiser, with unlimited mileage, from companies such as Fortes Safaris.

Zebras drinking

The right safari gear

Most travellers have been on a 'beach' holiday, perhaps several times, but for many the 'safari' is a novelty. What kind of gear do you need? What do you wear? What stuff do you need to take with you?

Vehicles

You may not think that 'which vehicle' is something you have to think about. However, there is a range of vehicles in which you might spend your week, and it could affect your holiday, so it is good to get it right. Many cheaper safari holidays, and especially those in Kenya, use Nissan or Toyota minibuses with only 2-wheel drive. During rains, you might well find yourselves outside pushing. On the slippery dirt mountain roads of Ngorongoro and Empakaai, there is also a safety issue.

Make sure you are going on safari in a good 4-wheel-drive vehicle, preferably a Land Rover or Land Cruiser. They are also higher, and give you better visibility.

Clothing

On the rim of Ngorongoro Crater, you will sleep at a height of about 2,300m (7,544ft), so temperatures are more like those in the UK than in Africa. Nights will be cool. During the day the thin air allows for intense solar radiation.

On safari one needs something warm for the evenings, but also clothing which is light and airy for the day. If you have pale skin, you might want to cover up your arms. The typical safari clothing you see in films and on TV is also quite sensible. All the pockets are great if you are a photographer, as most of us are in the bush.

Many people wear shorts, but if those pale legs have not seen light for some time, this is just the place to get a severe sunburn.

Wear a hat with a broad brim, even if you do feel a little bit silly. The sun can be very intense.

Boots, especially those sold in East Africa called 'safari' or 'desert' boots, are ideal for both sexes, as they protect the ankles from insects. They are also lightweight and cheap.

Creams, pills, injections etc.

There are insects that will bite you, and some are potentially serious, like mosquitoes. So do take anti-malarial pills as prescribed by your doctor or chemist. Start taking them according to the instructions *before* you leave home. Ask your doctor well in advance about the current need for inoculations, vaccinations etc.

Bring with you sufficient insect-repellent, something for insect bites like Anthisan, sufficient high-factor sun-block (remember the atmosphere is thinner and the radiation stronger at altitude) and a supply of whatever

On safari: the northern circuit

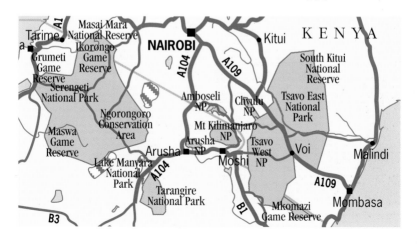

you take for a seriously upset stomach. This might include oral rehydration, as well as something like Imodium, especially when it is hot.

Also bring any other medicines that you would regard as normal. Remember that you will be away from civilisation during the time of your safari. Lodges and hotels in the wilderness will probably have limited things like paracetemol, adhesive plasters etc., but not much else.

Make sure your supplies of other prescription medicines will not run out during your safari.

Photographic supplies

Most of us are now digital photographers. However, film or digital, some things remain the same. Make sure you have enough batteries. Some lodges and camps have re-charging facilities, but by no means all.

If you are using film, make sure you bring more than enough, as supplies will be scarce, increasingly as digital photography takes over. And have a means of keeping your film cool, such as a cool bag, as high temperatures can ruin your pictures.

For both types of photography make sure you have a suitable zoom or telephoto lens. Something at least up to 300mm is required for many animal shots.

Books

Finally, you will get much more out of your safari if you read up before you go, and also if you come with the odd manual, depending on your level of expertise. Most people will benefit enormously from a decent bird book.

Serious safari transport vehicles

Typical safari tent

ARUSHA

Arusha is a crossroads – a meeting point of roads between Nairobi, Moshi and Dodoma. It has a mixture of people, local Arusha and Meru, together with Maasai and various Europeans, the most recent of whom have come to take part in the UN judicial process over the Rwanda massacres.

German colonialists developed Arusha as a military town in the late 19th century, but then it became more of a market town during the British period. The expected linkup with the railways to Dar es Salaam and to Kenya via Taveta and Voi never happened, and in the 1950s Arusha had a population of only 8,000. However, expansion since independence has been massive, mainly from rural-urban migration, and today's population is approaching half a million.

Arrival

Most visitors fly in, either through the new Kilimanjaro International Airport, or through Arusha Airport, which takes traffic from elsewhere in Tanzania.

If you fly in through Kilimanjaro International Airport, Arusha is likely to be your first stop. Some airlines such as KLM and their Tanzanian partner, Precision Air, have their own bus; almost all safari companies meet their clients at 'arrivals'. Arusha airport has the feeling of being a little chaotic. Make sure you are not separated from your baggage. As with many situations in Africa, you are immediately bombarded with men touting for your business, be it a taxi, a safari tour or a hotel.

There is a helpful **Tourist Board Office** located on Boma Road. If you do not have all your arrangements made, they can advise with a list of reputable safari tour companies, and also a list of those to avoid. Additionally on Boma Road is the Arusha office of the **Ngorongoro Conservation Area**, which controls access to the Ngorongoro Highlands, the Crater and Oldupai (formerly Olduvai). At the western edge of town, on the Dodoma to Manyara road, you will find the TANAPA (Tanzania National Parks Authority) Headquarters, who can also help with a variety of information, brochures and maps.

Arusha Town

The old colonial area of Arusha is relatively compact, and it contains most of the facilities that tourists might need. East of the centre, and beyond the Themi River, is the main upmarket housing area. To the south and the north lie the rapidly growing areas of

Cultural Heritage souvenir shop

low-quality housing that receive most of the new arrivals.

Try to get your bearings. Downtown Arusha is basically a gridiron pattern with Sokoine Road in the south, Makongoro Road in the middle and the Nairobi to Moshi road, which is almost a bypass, in the north. These all run east to west, and connecting streets run north to south. The eastern boundary of the commercial part of the town is the Themi River.

The National History Museum is located on Boma Road. It especially concentrates on the prehistorical importance of Tanzania as one of the likely 'cradles of mankind', and has a comprehensive display on Oldupai (formerly Olduvai).
Open: 9am–5pm. Admission charge.

The Arusha International Conference Centre is presently the venue for the International Criminal Tribunal for Rwanda, resulting in the explosion in the number of expatriates (and associated Land Cruisers) in the town.

The Arusha Declaration Museum is located at the junction of Uhuru Torch Roundabout (*Uhuru* means 'freedom'), and Makongoro Road. The museum mainly covers the colonial period and the declaration of the policy of *Ujamaa*, when villagers were forced to move from their traditional settlements to communist-inspired collective villages, a policy now generally abandoned and recognised as having been a social and economic disaster.

Open: 9.30am–5.30pm.
Admission charge.

The Central Market is located about 500m (550yds) south of the Arusha Declaration Museum. Markets are always good value for tourists. Apart from being the cheapest source for almost anything, they are also incredibly photogenic. Always remember to ask people before taking their photographs.

Tourist souvenir shops are places where many tourists start or finish their safari holiday, so there are inevitably lots of them around.

Cultural Heritage (and its adjacent art gallery) is the largest souvenir shop and has the biggest range. Located on Sokoine Road, at the western edge of town, it is your last stop before Manyara. It has secure parking, so you will not be hassled, but it is not the cheapest.

Lookmanji Curio Shop, located on Joel Maeda Street, has a good range and keen prices.

KAM Real Art Centre, located on Boma Road, mainly concentrates on Tingatinga art and batiks.

Arusha has lots of very good eating places covering all pockets and most tastes (*see Directory on p169*). In recent years, the Rwanda tribunal has encouraged a wider range of upmarket restaurants.

Arusha has a number of good hotels (*see Directory on p171*) and plenty of places where you can change money, though some banks may occasionally be short of foreign currency such as US dollars. ATMs may not always accept the full range of cards. You will also find that commission on traveller's cheques can verge on the criminal. It seems difficult for the tourist to be on the winning side when it comes to holiday money.

A luxury safari tent at Grumeti River Camp

On safari: the northern circuit

Safari tour operators

Arusha would compete with Nairobi as the safari tour centre of the world. It is certainly sensible to arrange your tour before you arrive, but if you haven't, there is a range of possibilities. Do not submit to the touts on the street who will offer all sorts of deals. Go to a reputable company which is on the Tourist Board list. Here are some examples:

- **Expensive tours:** Abercrombie & Kent and Greystoke Safaris.
- **Mid-range tours:** Fortes Safaris, Takim's Holidays and Hoopoe Adventure Tours. Hoopoe also organise hiking and trekking tours.
- **Budget tours:** Swala Safaris and Nature Discovery.

Safari lodges and camps

What can one expect from safari lodges and camps? Obviously lodges and camps vary, but if you go on a safari package tour, what you get is usually fairly consistent.

In safari camps, accommodation is normally in very large tents which stand on a permanent base. They will have en-suite facilities, sometimes separated from the tent by a wall, but sometimes only by a canvas screen.

You can expect running water at safari lodges and camps. Electricity may be available permanently, but more likely from about 6pm until about 11pm, and then again in the morning. It will come from a generator, or in more environmentally friendly

Ethnic architectural influences at Lake Manyara Serena Lodge

Mount Meru in the morning from Moivaro

locations, from photo-voltaic (solar) panels. Hot water may only be available in the evening, especially if it is heated by a wood burner or, again, by solar panels.

The large lodges often have rooms not too different from standard hotel rooms anywhere. Even if you are too high for malarial mosquitoes, both camps and lodges will usually have mosquito nets.

Public areas, the restaurant, bars and lounges in both camps and lodges conventionally take advantage of the view – overlooking the crater at Ngorongoro, out into the plains of Serengeti or over the edge of the Rift Valley at Manyara. Almost all have a pool, though some, even at the most exclusive end, do not. Check if it is important to you.

Food is usually international and of a high standard. In spite of stories about funny tummies in the tropics, hygiene is usually of an excellent standard, and you are no more likely to have tummy problems than in France or Greece.

Often there will be evening entertainment of Maasai singing and dancing, depending on the location of the lodge. Frequently there is also a tradition of a huge log fire, where you can sit outside before or after dinner and listen to the lions roaring or the sounds of the African night.

Usually there is a pattern of both morning and late afternoon/evening game drives. Also, it is possible to arrange a full day's safari with a packed lunch provided. This is especially so in huge areas such as Serengeti and Selous. In Tanzania, most game drives

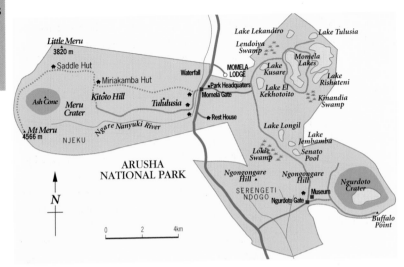

tend to be in specially converted Land Rovers or Land Cruisers.

Some camps and hotels, but not all, will have balloon trips. Places that do not have large areas of open grassland for landing, such as Manyara, cannot have balloons. Drifting over the savannah in the still morning light is the experience of a lifetime. Though it is an expensive addition, it will be a memorable highlight of your safari.

ARUSHA NATIONAL PARK

The chances are that you or your tour guide will be in such a rush to reach Ngorongoro or Serengeti that you will sail straight past Arusha National Park. However, if you can spare the time, it is definitely worth a visit. The park is very close to Arusha, the name coming from the Warusa people who traditionally live in the area.

At only 137sq km (53sq miles),

Arusha is one of the smallest national parks. However, within that small area it boasts a wide range of habitats, including high montane forest and a collection of lakes full of waterbirds. The park is wrapped around Mount Meru, which dominates the Arusha skyline to the north. Meru is the fifth highest peak in Africa, and the second in Tanzania after Kilimanjaro. There is also a range of beautiful butterflies, especially in the forest (*see box on p48*).

The Ngurdoto Gate, the entrance to the park, is about one hour from Arusha, and it is possible to drive through the park via Ngurdoto Crater and then on to Lokie Swamp and the lakes Longil and Jembamba. There are three distinct ecozones within the park, starting with the Ngurdoto Crater in the southeast. Secondly there are the Momela lakes in the northeast, with Momela itself at 1,500m (4,921ft).

Finally there is the summit of Meru, rising to 4,566m (14,980ft).

Vegetation relates to both altitude and geology. Ngurdoto is forest and swamp, and the Momela lakes are alkaline-soda. The lower slopes of the summit of Meru are forest, whereas the summit itself is bare rock.

Along the way you are likely to see a wide range of animals, including buffalo, zebra, giraffe, warthog and many others. Look up to the canopy for the shy black-and-white colobus monkeys.

In contrast with most national parks, it is possible to have a walking safari, as long as you have a ranger-guide.

MANYARA
The drive west to Manyara

It is a good idea to think of the drive (and there may be quite a lot of driving on your safari) as part of your holiday. The road to Manyara and Ngorongoro, recently built with Japanese aid, is superb by African standards. It is now

Female black rhino

tarred all the way to the Ngorongoro Gate. The road leaves Arusha through groves of coffee plantations, quickly leaving the bustle of the town behind. Savannah grassland takes over quite abruptly from woodland, with views to volcanoes such as **Kitumbeine** and **Burko** on the horizon.

Strangely, herds of camels graze by the road, and in some places overgrazing has resulted in serious soil erosion, with much of the surface soil washed away.

Look out for 'sleeping policemen' or traffic humps, especially approaching schools and villages. Usually you are given warning but not always.

At the Makuyuni junction you turn right for **Manyara** on to a superb piece of new road. However, watch out for 'drifts', suddenly appearing concrete drainage channels across the road, which can take you completely by surprise, especially when you are driving fast.

The eastern wall of the **Great Rift Valley** and the shimmer of **Lake Manyara** begin to appear in the distance, with the massif of the Ngorongoro Highlands further behind. About two hours from Arusha you arrive in the small town of **Mto Wa Mbu** at the foot of the escarpment, where there is a nice range of Maasai gifts.

LAKE MANYARA NATIONAL PARK
Lake Manyara National Park is the first park on the northern safari route,

which ultimately ends in Serengeti. At 330sq km (127sq miles), it is small, but a visit to Manyara contains much of the essence of the traditional African safari. It lies at the foot of the western escarpment wall of the Great Rift Valley, just beyond the township of **Mto Wa Mbu**. As you approach Manyara from Arusha, there is little to see of the eastern edge of the valley, but the western wall is clearly visible, with the fertile highlands of Mbululand above it. Beyond that are the **Ngorongoro Highlands** clad in rainforest, and often in cloud.

The park has a wide range of habitats. Forest survives near the escarpment due to springs which well up and supplement the 700mm (28in) of annual rainfall. Further out from the slope there is acacia woodland, and then the swamps and eventually the lake itself.

Manyara has traditionally enjoyed high animal densities, especially of elephant and lions, with elephants now recovering from heavy poaching in the 1970s and 80s. Manyara lions are not the only tree-climbers, but they are probably the most famous. The park has large herds of buffalo and a range of antelopes, together with almost 400 recorded bird species.

Sadly, Manyara is also a microcosm of one other major problem, the local extinction of species due to population pressure. In recent years, numerous previously common animals have disappeared from the park, including black rhino, African hunting dogs and cheetah.

An excellent road with the Rift Valley escarpment in the distance

Manyara is small enough for a day trip, and is popular with the increasing number of expatriates now living in Arusha. The roads are suitable for 2-wheel-drive vehicles, but almost everyone comes in a 4×4.

For birders, the best time is the November to June wet season; for animals it is best to view them in the dry season.

To the west and south of the lake is evidence that this is still an active volcanic area, in the form of hot springs **Maji Moto Ndogo** and **Maji Moto Kubwa** (literally 'little' and 'big' hot water). Springs bubble to the surface with temperatures up to 76°C (169°F).

The tourist accommodation is nearly all outside the park, but only a few minutes away from the single entrance. There are two lodges and one tented

Masai giraffe

camp, all perched on the edge of the escarpment providing superb views. The new E Unoto Retreat is about 10km (6 miles) away, nestled at the base of the escarpment to the north.

On safari: the northern circuit

Swimming pool at Manyara overlooking the Great Rift Valley

MASAI GIRAFFE

The Masai giraffe (*Giraffa camelopardalis tippelskirchi*) is the tallest mammal, reaching 5.5m (18ft). Bulls can be a metre (3ft) higher than females. They weigh 1,100–1,900kg (2,425–4,189lb).

There are eight species of giraffe. The Masai giraffe found in many areas of East Africa has the most irregular pattern of markings and colour variation.

The giraffe generally eats within a 2m (6$\frac{1}{2}$ft) range from 3–5m (10–16ft) above the ground. They are non-territorial, living in loose, open herds.

Fifty per cent of calves are killed by lions and hyenas, in spite of the mother's valiant efforts to protect them.

The Maasai

Who are the Maasai?

Undoubtedly the image of the Maasai is the best known of all the peoples of East Africa. Everyone knows of the tall and handsome warriors dressed in bright red blankets and carrying spears. But who are these noble people?

The word *maasai* comes from the word *maa*, which is the language of the Maasai. So the Maasai are the people who speak Maa.

They came to Tanzania late, indeed the very last of all the major tribes, a mere 200–300 years ago, probably arriving in the area in the early 19th

Maasai cattle on the road to Empakaai

century, having begun to leave their original homeland in the Nile region of southern Sudan perhaps 500 years ago. They are traditionally a warrior people, and as they arrived, they displaced others like the Datoga who had been here for several hundred years.

The Maasai and cattle

Above all the Maasai are cattle herders; every part of their lives is associated with cattle, and cattle are the main sign of wealth. Maasai religion tells them that God (Ngai) gave all cattle on Earth to the Maasai for them to keep and look after, when he passed them down from Heaven to Earth. Traditionally, Maasai cattle-raiding was justified simply as rounding up of animals that had strayed, but were actually their property, according to their beliefs.

Maasai family near Empakaai

Maasai are not hunters, and traditionally live in harmony with wild animals. They get almost all their needs from cattle: meat, milk, blood, hides and, as building material for their homes, dung.

Traditionally Maasai have been semi-nomadic, migrating between pastures depending on the rains, and often between the high and low ground. Today, as population pressure and increased fencing of land make the nomadic way of life more difficult, this traditional part of their lives is under threat.

Maasai girl near Kiloki

The Maasai village

Maasai live in small villages called *enkang*, though often the word *manyatta* is used by tourists. Each *enkang* is located within a thorn fence, mainly to deter predators such as lions from attacking the cattle. The houses are made by the women from sticks and cow dung.

The *manyatta* is technically the village where the young Maasai warriors live during their years as *morani* (warriors) before they become tribal elders. Usually it is separate, but not far from the main village.

Traditions

Although ways of life are being eroded, the Maasai are still fiercely traditional. Many are very well educated and go to high school and university, but they are fiercely proud, retain their language, their dress and above all their belief in the importance of cattle.

Maasai and wildlife

The Maasai no longer live within the national parks, but within regions like the Ngorongoro Conservation Area. Here they retain watering rights, even on the crater floor. As they have never been hunters, many Maasai believe there is no conflict between the Maasai way of living and the survival of wildlife. However, the ever-increasing population pressure makes it absolutely essential that those living around, or adjacent to, wildlife locations also have a clear and serious financial interest in them.

Walk: climbing Mount Meru

Meru (Ol Doinyo Orok, 'the Black Mountain' in Maasai) is the second-highest mountain in Tanzania and the fifth highest in Africa. Though not totally without the problems of altitude sickness most witnessed on Kilimanjaro, it is generally a much easier climb. It can be done in three days, but most climbers take four. It is not a technical climb and can be described as a 'tough walk'.

You are likely to encounter a wide range of wildlife while climbing Mount Meru, including giraffe, various species of monkey, duikers and other antelope, and buffalo. It is a great location for bird watching, with almost 600 species of birds recorded. A ranger-guide, obtainable at the Momela Gate Park headquarters, is obligatory, though many who climb Mount Meru do not join a formal expedition as they would on Kilimanjaro. To be safe, use one of numerous safari companies based in Arusha with plenty of experience of the climb.

Day One – The Gate to Mirakamba Hut
The route starts at about 1,500m (4,921ft) at the **Momela Gate**, and the first day takes you up and into the rainforest, which starts at about 1,800m (5,906ft) and follows the more southerly of two possible routes. The walk passes the Itikoni clearing, popular with buffalo, and the Tululusia Waterfall on the Tululusia River. At

Floral and open road from Arusha to Lake Manyara

Njeku there is a fine view over the **Momela lakes** to the east. **Mirakamba Hut** is reached at 2,600m (8,530ft), just below the top edge of the forest.

Day Two – Mirakamba Hut to Saddle Hut
After leaving the Mirakamba Hut, it is only a 300m (984ft) climb until you are out of the rainforest and on to open moorland heading for **Saddle Hut** at 3,600m (11,811ft), with the route following Elephant Ridge.

To the north is **Little Meru**, 750m (2,461ft) lower than the summit.

Day Three – Acclimatisation and Little Meru

One way of acclimatising is to use Day 3 to climb Little Meru, 3,820m (12,533ft) – a walk of approximately 5 or 6 hours.

Day Four – Summit and descent to Saddle or Mirakamba Huts

From Saddle Hut to the **summit** at 4,566m (14,980ft) takes about 6 hours along the western rim of the crater. Leave around midnight to aim for a lovely sunrise over Kilimanjaro 80km (50 miles) to the east.

From leaving the summit at dawn, it is possible to go all the way to the gate by mid-afternoon, but many take their time and stay over at one of the huts on the way down, so going into a fifth day.

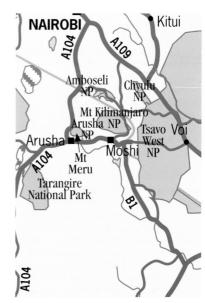

Mount Meru from Lake Duluti

The Great Rift Valley

The Great Rift Valley is one of the most outstanding geological features on Earth. It runs from southern Lebanon, through the Dead Sea, into the Red Sea and the Ethiopian Highlands. In the north of East Africa it splits into two arms, the western section going through western Uganda, and eventually running into Lake Tanganyika, the second-deepest lake in the world. The eastern arm follows Lake Turkana and then moves south through the highlands of Kenya, west of Nairobi, and then along the line of small lakes, Magadi, Natron, Manyara and Eyasi. At times the line of the valley is confused, but ultimately the two arms rejoin in southern Tanzania to form Lake Nyasa, eventually to end near the mouth of the Zambezi River.

Sandwiched between is Lake Victoria, the world's second-largest freshwater lake. It is believed to be geologically very young, perhaps only a few thousand years old.

You will most likely encounter the Great Rift Valley on your journey to Ngorongoro and Serengeti, especially the dramatic valley walls at Lakes Manyara and Eyasi. All around are volcanoes – **Kilimanjaro**, the world's largest free-standing mountain, **Ngorongoro**, the largest continuous caldera in the world, once perhaps 6,000m (19,685ft) high, and **Ol Doinyo Lengai**, the Maasai 'Mountain of the Gods', currently the most active volcano in East Africa.

It is a veritable feast of volcanic scenery.

Western edge of the Rift Valley at E Unoto

Ol Doinyo Lengai volcano

Origins of the Rift Valley

During the last 30–40 years the Theory of Plate Tectonics has given us an explanation of why the Earth's major features are located where they are. Huge crustal plates are moved by convection forces deep underground. At the plate boundaries, the plates are either moving apart or colliding. Usually plates move apart in the middle of the oceans, but in a few places this happens on land.

It is believed that Africa is one of these places, and that the Great Rift Valley is witness to Africa literally tearing itself apart. For hundreds of millions of years, Africa has been geologically stable, but now the eastern section is heading off across the Indian Ocean, perhaps, in 50 million years' time, to collide with India and form a new Himalayas. In the valleys at Manyara and Lake Eyasi we can see this process beginning.

As the split began to occur, a huge crack, perhaps 8,000km (4,970 miles) long, appeared. Just as submarine rifts give rise to volcanoes under the sea in the Atlantic, so we find active or recent volcanoes either on the floor of the Great Rift Valley or close to it.

Most volcanoes are the product of the last 20 million years, almost the present in a world deemed to be 4,500 million years old.

Mount Meru, near Arusha, last erupted about 200 years ago and is regarded as dormant, the Kibo summit of Kilimanjaro has active fumaroles, while Ol Doinyo Lengai erupts regularly, every few decades or so, and most recently in 1983. So the process continues; the valley will widen and as old volcanoes become extinct and eroded, new ones will emerge where presently there is only plain. Then, after a few tens of millions of years, there will be a new continent off the coast of East Africa.

Ngorongoro Crater and Conservation Area

From the top of the escarpment to the gate of the Ngorongoro Conservation Area, you travel on a superb new road through rich volcanic farmland, where mainly maize is grown. It was in the late 1950s that the German zoologist father-and-son team Bernhard and Michael Grzimek first recognised Ngorongoro, together with the Serengeti Plains, as one of the very special animal environments of the world. Few people who visit the area can remain unmoved by its amazing spectacle.

The business of paying for permits at the Ngorongoro Conservation Area gate seems to take an age as all the Land Cruisers and Land Rovers from Arusha appear to arrive at the same time from mid- to late morning. Use this time to buy a map and orientate yourself.

The route to the crater rim is now on a *murram* (dirt) road, and soon enters the rainforest, an environment of cooler temperatures and high humidity. The deeply entrenched valleys are clothed with an enormous variety of trees, some with clean, smooth trunks, extending to the sky, and others clad in creepers and ivies, hitching a ride to the sunlight. On your left is an increasingly long and steep slope, as you climb higher and higher to the top of the volcano.

At an altitude of just over 2,200m (7,218ft), there is a break in the forest and usually a huddle of vehicles, and you can see into the crater for the first time. The initial view is difficult to take in. 'Where are the animals?' is the usual first thought, as you battle to comprehend the scale of the view, firstly 600m (1,969ft) to the crater floor and then 20km (12 miles) from west to east, the size of a large city. Most obvious is **Lake Magadi**, at the western end, the green of **Lerai Forest** next to

NGORONGORO HIGHLANDS BUTTERFLIES

The rainforest is the best place for butterflies, and if you choose to trek in the Ngorongoro Highlands, for example to Olmuti or Empakaai, you can observe them closely.

Ngorongoro Highlands are great for butterflies

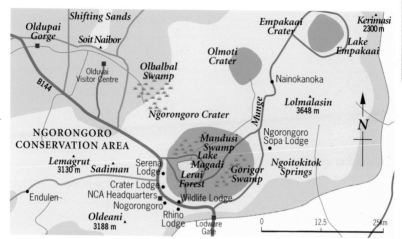

it, and then the unbroken crater walls, making Ngorongoro the largest continuous volcanic crater in the world. Then you adjust to the hundreds of tiny dots scattered throughout the plains, each group representing great grazing herds of wildebeest, buffalo and zebra, among the 30,000 large mammals living here at any one time.

Allow yourself time to soak in the spectacle and to become adjusted to the vastness of Ngorongoro, before you move on. If you are staying at **Sopa Lodge**, you need to turn right and drive anticlockwise around the rim; for everywhere else, including Serengeti and Oldupai (formerly Olduvai), turn left and drive clockwise. The journey through the rainforest, along the winding track that follows the ridge, takes about another 30 minutes.

The descent to the crater floor

There are three access roads. The descent is normally from Windy Gap, down the Seneto or western wall. The ascent is normally made from Lerai Forest, below Ngorongoro Wildlife Lodge. The road from the eastern rim allows both descent and ascent for Sopa Lodge and the numerous campsites in that area.

The Seneto descent of about 600m (1,969ft) is surprisingly gentle, with only one hairpin bend, and no real sensation of being 'exposed' on the crater wall. It takes about 15 minutes.

The most obvious feature on the descent is the shallow Lake Magadi (a soda lake), the size of which varies with the seasons. At the end of the dry season, the water is reduced to a small, central lake, surrounded by soda flats. In the rains, the lake expands to about 5km (3 miles) east to west. On the water, as with all the soda lakes in the area, there are large flocks of lesser flamingos and pelicans.

Lerai Forest and Lake Magadi, Ngorongoro Crater

Next to the lake you will find the forest called Lerai by the Maasai. This is the Maa word for *Acacia xanthophloea*, the yellow-barked 'fever tree'. In the forest one will see woodland dwellers and browsers such as waterbuck, elephant and black rhino.

Most of Ngorongoro's animals are grazers, and include wildebeest, buffalo, zebra and Thomson's and Grant's gazelles, as well as eland, kongoni and many warthogs, which seem less timid here than elsewhere. There are numerous hippo pools and about 20 black rhinos. Rhinos are presently recovering from a serious collapse in their numbers due to poaching. From well over 100 rhinos in the crater in the 1960s, numbers once plummeted to fewer than 10. Today a vigorous rhino project keeps tabs on every animal, and poaching seems to have been wiped out.

A small group of elephant moves between woodland and open grassland.

Ngorongoro has more of the big cats to the square kilometre than anywhere else in Africa. So almost everyone gets to see lions and cheetah, as well as other predators such as hyena and jackal. There are many leopards, but they are secretive and more difficult to see.

There are several picnic sites, but otherwise you may not get out of your vehicle.

Throughout the crater floor there are elevated positions which afford a good lookout, where you can spy out the land and plan your next game-drive. **Eldoinyo Engitati** has a small ridge, allowing you to look out over the plains in the northern crater floor.

Some guidebooks suggest that a day is enough time in Ngorongoro, but it is the author's long experience that a relaxed and patient period of game viewing, even just staying in one or two places, can be enormously rewarding.

At one time it was even possible to camp in the crater, and indeed there were several Maasai *bomas*, and in colonial times a European farm, but today everyone must be out by 6pm. So plan your trip with plenty of time. The ascent late in the day can have spectacular light, with long shadows, and this can be the best time to get the most favourable impression of the crater.

Empakaai

Empakaai is one of the volcanic cones northwest of Ngorongoro, and it is well worth the half day it takes to visit. The journey follows the eastern rim of Ngorongoro, through rainforest of enormous trees and creepers, past Sopa

Lodge and the start of the eastern route into the crater.

The road soon emerges into grassland, and one can see first the volcano **Olmoti**, and then **Empakaai** in the distance, perhaps 10km (6 miles) away. The landscape for most of the rest of the journey is one of rolling, open grassland, with huge herds of Maasai cattle, sheep and goats, together with the biggest flocks of donkeys you might see anywhere. Villages are scattered about the hillsides in the shadow of volcanic cones, and the people here seem much less affected by tourism than elsewhere. There are almost no other vehicles – perhaps only two or three in a whole day.

Eventually the road re-enters the rainforest, and after a kilometre or so, you are on the rim of the Empakaai crater, a few hundred metres higher than Ngorongoro and with a view almost 1,000m (328ft) down to a brilliant turquoise lake. It is an amazing sight, with the crater walls lined with rainforest to the bottom, and the edge of the lake rimmed with the brilliant pink of thousands of lesser flamingos, the noise of which drifts up to the crater rim like that of a seabird-cliff in Scotland or Norway during the breeding season.

Oldupai (formerly Olduvai)

Oldupai comes from the Maasai word for wild sisal, which grows in the Oldupai Gorge, about 30km (19 miles) from Ngorongoro Crater, and about one hour's drive from Crater and Serena lodges. Oldupai is one of the world's most famous archaeological sites.

Although all the tour guides know exactly where the gorge is located, at the time of the author's visit there were no signposts to this famous location, coming from either Ngorongoro or Serengeti. However, if you head out from Ngorongoro on the Serengeti road, past the crater descent road, you will pass, in about 12km (7 miles), the **Loonkoka Cultural Boma**, just off the road to the right. A further 12km (7 miles) and tracks begin to head off to the right. Follow these and you will arrive at **Oldupai** in about 6km (3³/₄ miles). Eventually, it is difficult to miss, as the gorge blocks your path.

There is a small museum, full of interesting copies of the most important finds, and helpful guides who will give a short introductory talk and conduct tours into the gorge to examine recent excavations. There are also toilets and a gift shop. There are other claims to the most likely origins of man, but it is nice to know that this is possibly where we all came from.

Oldupai Gorge

Ngorongoro Crater and Conservation Area

Ngorongoro, eighth Wonder of the World

You will read in many texts the description 'Ngorongoro, eighth Wonder of the World'; in another, 'arguably the most famous wildlife refuge in the world'. This is a truly magical place, and for many the highlight of their visit to Africa. The first view into the crater, at the top of the drive through Oldeani Forest, is truly memorable (*see also pp48–9*).

Ngorongoro ascent road through the rainforest

History

For centuries Ngorongoro Crater was occupied by a succession of hunter-gatherers, hunters, pastoralists and then farmers. The Dorobo people were followed by the Barbaig, who were themselves displaced by the Maasai. In 1892, the first European to see the crater was the Austrian Oscar Baumann.

It became a game reserve, with some measure of control on hunting in 1921, and in 1951 became part of Serengeti National Park. In 1959, the Ngorongoro Conservation Area, 8,300sq km (3,205sq miles), was formed, and initially it was declared a 'multiple land-use area', with Maasai cattle and wild animals sharing the grazing. When the writer first visited the crater in 1964, there were two villages, and Maasai *bomas* remained until 1974, cattle eventually being excluded in the 1990s. Maasai herders still retain some watering rights.

Geology

Ngorongoro is part of a group of extinct, dormant and active volcanoes associated with the widening of the Great Rift Valley of Africa. At one time it was probably as high as Kilimanjaro. Today it is the world's biggest unbroken crater or 'caldera', which is up to 19km (12 miles) in diameter, and stands at over 2,500m

(8,200ft), so the lodges on the rim are located at approximately this height. The crater walls are 600m (1,969ft) high.

Calderas are generally formed in two ways. One is that the volcano 'blows its top' as with Mount St Helens in USA in 1980, or Krakatoa more dramatically in 1883. Alternatively, and most likely with Ngorongoro, the central cone of the volcano simply collapsed into the magma chamber below. In the case of Krakatoa, sea water rushed in and there was a mighty explosion, but with Ngorongoro it left us with the continuous crater we still have today.

Ngorongoro is part of a series of volcanoes in the area. A few kilometres to the north are the cones of Empakaai and Olmoti, from which the Munge River flows to provide Ngorongoro's main fresh-water source. To the south is Mount Oldeani, at 3,216m (10,551ft) the highest peak in the Ngorongoro Highlands. Further away to the north is Ol Doinyo Lengai, East Africa's most active volcano, which last erupted in 1993.

As with most big mountains in East Africa, Ngorongoro exhibits a range of vegetation which is controlled mainly by altitude and rainfall. As you approach from Karatu in the south, the rich farmlands suddenly give way to the rainforests of the Northern Highlands Forest Reserve, which clothe the eastern and southern slopes, and also down into the crater. The western and northern slopes are generally drier and are mainly grassland.

On the crater floor the vegetation varies from the salt-desert around Lake Magadi, to the grasslands covering most of the low ground, to the swamp vegetation of Gorigor and Mandusi.

Evening view from Crater Lodge

Serengeti National Park, World Heritage Site

Serengeti is quite simply one of the world's most famous and important wildlife locations. First brought to the world's attention by German zoologists Bernhard Grzimek and his son Michael, the Serengeti National Park is at the core of a 28,000sq km (10,811sq mile) ecosystem that sees more than two million animals migrating through it annually.

Unless you fly, you will most likely approach Serengeti via Ngorongoro and probably Oldupai. Even if you miss out Ngorongoro Crater on the way there, you will still most likely travel through the Ngorongoro Highlands and down towards Oldupai (formerly Olduvai) Gorge.

A series of braided tracks heads off from Oldupai (formerly Olduvai) and rejoins the road to Serengeti near the **Kiloki Cultural Boma**.

There are frequently no signposts, so if you are unsure, follow a 4×4 with a

Serengeti, Maasai for 'never-ending plains'

tour-guide driver heading in the same direction. Once you reach the main road, turn right, and after about 20km (12 miles) you pass into the park through a 'Welcome to Serengeti' gate, and you have arrived in a protected wildlife area bigger than many countries. If you are an independent traveller, do take navigation seriously; if you take a wrong turn it may be 30–50km (19–31 miles) before you see anything that tells you so.

Serengeti is huge, so you will not find lodges and campsites everywhere. However, many visitors concentrate on the main 'hotspots' of **Seronera**, the **Western Corridor** and **Lobo**.

Wherever you do your game viewing, pay special attention around the numerous *kopjes*. *Kopjes* are the archetypal landscape feature of Serengeti. They are made of low hills of weathered granite boulders and occur in clusters around the national park. As you approach from the south, the first major ones are the **Simba Kopjes** about 20km (12 miles) north of the **Naabi Hill Gate**.

Where there are continuous plains, any change in the landscape offers shade, a viewpoint and, for females, a place to have their young. So the *kopjes* are among the main game-viewing sites. Linger there and spend some time. Even if you do not see something immediately, there will be animal eyes looking out at you. You may see lions resting up there, and if you are lucky, a leopard.

Serengeti lions

Knowing a little information about the social life of lions will make your lion-viewing more interesting. Serengeti is one of the best places on Earth to view lions. There are over 3,000 of

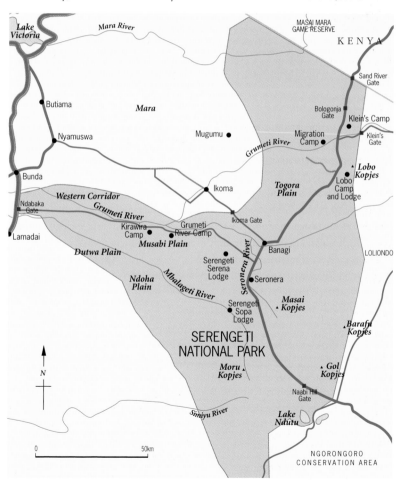

Serengeti lions are magnificent

them in the national park, and the short grasses make lion-viewing such that almost every visitor is guaranteed to see them.

Lions are sociable cats that live in groups called prides. They co-operate in many of the things they do, especially bringing up their young and in hunting. Most other cats, such as leopards and even cheetahs, are relatively solitary, the biggest group normally being mother and her young. Some prides number over 30 lions.

A pride consists of related females, their cubs and one or more pride males. They live in a territory, in which they stay, and which they will defend against other neighbouring prides. In general, lion prides do not move with the herds as has been suggested by some authorities.

Females generally stay with the pride

for the whole of their lives, and usually live longer than males. Male lions are expelled from the pride when they reach puberty, and they must then make their own way in the world, often two brothers linking up to make a

LION

Lions (*Panthera leo*) (Swahili: *Simba*) weigh 190–250kg (419–551lb) and stand 110–120cm (43–47in) tall. They are fully developed by about five years old. Male lions have a hard life fighting to retain their pride and usually die before they are ten. Females live longer, to about fifteen.

Lions are the most numerous predators after the spotted hyena.

Males often make a power coalition with their brother(s), so becoming more successful. Females usually have a litter of cubs every two years. Often the whole pride synchronises the arrival of cubs, which gives them a better chance of survival.

formidable team. Male lions must fight to take over a pride and then to defend it. Two lions are more effective than one. However, lions are very rarely masters of a group of females for more than a year or two, and as a result of violent and inevitably fatal fights with other males, they do not live long.

Lions are most effective as a unit when they are hunting, which may be every day or every few days, usually at night. The hunting is done mainly by the female lions. Prey depends on the season, with wildebeest and zebra on the menu during the migrations, and the resident animals such as topi, buffalo, eland and impala being hunted during the rest of the year. The hunt is carried out by a group, and certainly appears to be according to a plan, where different animals each have their own function during the hunt. Large prides find it much easier to tackle a buffalo, and such a hunt might involve four or five lions eventually bringing down the animal. They generally kill by suffocating their prey with a bite to the neck or even over its entire snout.

If they are nearby, the males will eat first, then the females, and lastly the cubs. Almost as soon as the kill is made, other predators drawn by the commotion of the hunt will be on the scene, especially spotted hyenas and silver-backed jackals. Although a group of hyenas is no match for a large pride of lions, it is quite normal for a large group to drive small groups of lions or individuals from the kill. Finally, when there is not much left, the scavenging birds will arrive, including the lappet-faced vulture, Ruppell's griffon vulture and the maribou stork. After a short while there will be almost nothing left.

Then the lions go to sleep to rest and digest their enormous meal. Many visitors find it frustrating that the lions are not more active. However, the truth is that lions spend most of their time doing not very much.

View of Serengeti from Sopa Lodge

Where to find lions

Lions rest in particular places. They do not normally prefer to lie out in the open without shade from the hot sun. So look in areas of shade, in clumps of bushes, under isolated trees, along riverbeds and stream beds with some thicket for cover, or among the frequent *kopjes* that are dotted around Serengeti.

During the rains, prey species may be anywhere, but during the dry season they must go to where there is water. The lions know this too, so their dry season hunting ground may be much more localised than in the rains. Concentrate on waterholes, streams and rivers, especially during evening game drives and in the early morning, and you will discover the thrill of lion-watching.

Serengeti – one park, many locations

Because Serengeti is so big, you shouldn't think of it as one location, but as many different places. Lodges and campsites occur in clusters, each with its own airstrip and selection of game drives. In many ways, each also has its own season.

Lake Ndutu is in the extreme south and has a cluster of five or six camps. The migration comes here in January to April when wildebeest and zebra have their young.

Moru Kopjes is just a little further north and enjoys the same migration pattern, but is also a good location for big cats.

Seronera is in the centre and benefits from being at the crossroads, with year-round interest. It also has the most resident animals.

Lobo is in the northeast and has only a few camps to enjoy migrations from November to December and again from April to May.

The **Grumeti River**, **Kirawira** and the **Mbalagati River** areas are all in the western corridor. As well as enjoying the April to July migrations, they also benefit from the wealth of animals drawn to permanent water during the dry season.

THOMSON'S GAZELLE

The Thomson's gazelle (*Gazella thomsoni*) is 60–90cm (24–35in) tall and both sexes have horns. It is distinguished from Grant's gazelle by being smaller, and having a distinctive black side stripe and a black nose.

Females reach reproductive state in nine months. They often have two calves a year.

Herds usually number up to about 200. They make up the third most important element of the migrations, after wildebeest and zebra.

Thomson's gazelle

Ethnic architecture, Serengeti Serena

Seronera

The Seronera area is located right in the centre of the national park on the Seronera River. It is the best year-round game viewing area. It catches the southerly migrations in November and December, and also the northward and westward movements in March, April and May. There are also lots of resident species such as impala, topi, waterbuck, giraffe and eland still there when the migrants have passed. It benefits in numbers of species because of its location, at a boundary between the habitats of the southern plains of the south and the woodlands of the north. Along the river there is a wealth of hippos and crocodiles, and over 500 recorded species of birds.

Do not miss out on the **Serengeti Visitor Centre**, located at Seronera, which provides an imaginative display explaining the wonders of Serengeti and its history as a national park. Also enjoy the sound effects, with roaring lions pervading every space.

The Serengeti National Park Headquarters and the offices of the Frankfurt Zoological Society's ongoing project are also nearby.

Seronera is also the place to try ballooning. To balloon over the African savannah is something everyone should aim to experience at least once; it is an experience like no other. You start by getting up long before sunrise to a warming mug of tea or coffee, and driving to the take-off site. The balloon is still lying on the ground, usually tethered to a heavy tractor. The inflation with hot air will already have started, and gradually the multi-coloured fabric rises and becomes a huge, floating object above you. Usually there is room

Markus Borner heads Frankfurt Zoo's work in Serengeti

for 12–16 passengers; you all climb in, and after a few more short 'burns', the balloon slowly leaves the ground and you enter a whole new realm.

Except for the occasional burn, you drift silently over trees and bushes, and out over the 'never-ending plains' of Serengeti, initially high over the herds of grazers. You may see a large pride of lions or a small family group of cheetah. Approaching the Masai Kopjes, the pilot allows the balloon to drift down near the ground to spy out lions resting among the boulders. The flight ends with a bit of a bump, soon forgotten in the experience of a champagne breakfast, prepared by the crew who have been following your flight from the ground.

FRANKFURT ZOOLOGICAL SOCIETY

Frankfurt Zoological Society has been at the forefront of research and promotion of conservation in Serengeti since the 1950s, and research projects continue today from a centre at Seronera. Bernhard Grzimek and his son Michael started the work in the 1950s, and awakened the world to the need to protect Serengeti with their book, *Serengeti Shall Not Die*, published by Hamish Hamilton in 1960, and subsequently made into a film.

Today the work continues under the direction of Markus Borner, who succeeded Bernhard Grzimek, and who is already into his third decade in Serengeti.

There is a memorial to the Grzimeks on the southern rim of Ngorongoro crater. Michael died when his plane crashed into a vulture in the Gol Mountains.

The western corridor

This corridor extends westwards from Seronera towards Lake Victoria, with Grumeti Controlled Area to the north and Maswa Game Reserve to the south. Visit the Corridor in May to July, when the migrations are heading through the area, north to Masai Mara. The crossing of the Grumeti River can be similar to that of the more famous Mara River. It too has its huge crocodiles, hundreds of hippo and attendant predators and hangers-on in the vicinity of the crossing points.

Lobo

Lobo Kopjes in the northeast are another special location, lying as they do across both the migration routes in July to September, when animals are moving north, and again in November to December, when they come home to Tanzania. And all the time there are the residents such as impala, topi, eland, buffalo, lion and elephant.

Cheetahs – the fastest land mammals

Staying outside the national park

If you stay outside the national park, often the game viewing is just as good, but it is possible to go on night game drives and to have walking safaris, both usually not allowed by TANAPA. At night you can see a whole different range of animals, including aardvark, ratel, serval, genet, side-striped jackal, African wildcat, civet and porcupine.

Walking safaris can range from just a few hours to several days, using 'flycamps' each night.

The African night

Many who live in cities in Africa, or indeed anywhere in the world, are dazzled at night by lights, and never ever see the sky and the stars in all their sparkling clarity. Out in the bush, especially in a simple campsite, there are no lights, anywhere. At some camps, such as **Ikoma**, not only are you positively encouraged to enjoy the African night, but they also have a camp telescope to view whatever is out there.

Gold in the hills

From Ikoma it is also possible to visit an old, traditional goldmine at **Nyagoti**, abandoned a hundred years ago, and about an hour from the camp.

CHEETAH

The cheetah (*Acinonyx jubatas*) weighs 35–60kg (77–132lb) and is about 80cm (31in) in height.

It is best known as the fastest mammal on the planet, being able to sustain speeds of about 110kph (68mph) for short periods.

They live relatively solitary lives – a mother with her cubs or small groups of brothers. They hunt by day in the open savannah, taking small antelopes or the young of larger animals.

They are under threat of local extinction in many areas. Tourist pressure (lots of vehicles crowding an animal trying to hunt) is a serious problem. Give cheetahs space.

The great migration

'Everyone who has a chance to see nearly two million animals on the move has been touched by the magic of this place. What is it that gets under our skin? The urgency of the movement of the wildebeest? The wide, open plains? The African light? Or maybe the fact that we all came from here, not such a long time ago, and our deep unconsciousness remembers the time 6,000 generations ago … Or maybe it is just the sheer numbers of migrating animals as they move in the world's last great surviving migration.'

Markus Borner, Frankfurt Zoological Society's main representative in Serengeti.

It was in the late 1950s that father and son zoologists Bernhard and Michael Grzimek from Frankfurt Zoo in Germany first attempted to count the animals in the annual migration of wildebeest, zebra and Thomson's gazelle around the Serengeti-Masai Mara ecosystem. They announced it to the world in the book *Serengeti Shall Not Die* and in the subsequent film. The present existence of the Serengeti National Park owes much to them.

Michael died during the work, when his plane collided with a vulture.

What is the migration pattern?

The migrations are never identical and vary every year and over time. However, there is a basic pattern to the movements, largely affected by availability of water.

The wildebeest have their calves between December and May on the nutrient-rich grasses of southeast Serengeti and the Ngorongoro Conservation Area. Here volcanic ash makes a nutrient-rich hard pan, difficult for trees and bushes to penetrate, but where grasses are in their element. As the plains begin to dry out, the animals start to move west and then northwards into the area called the Western Corridor, where they stay until June or early July. Then two million animals move northwards, plodding in single-file lines towards the north, eventually ending up north of the Kenyan border

Male wildebeest fighting for territory

in the better-watered Masai Mara, where they stay until October or November. Then they move, with equal purpose, back to the southeast Serengeti Plains to begin the cycle over again.

The migrating animals form the seasonal prey for over 3,000 lions and large numbers of leopard, cheetah and other predators.

Is there a social structure in the migration?

Who leads the way? Who decides? One would imagine that such a massive movement of animals would require some great social order. However, apart from the relationship between mother and calf, wildebeest appear to have no family ties, or even a leader. 'Any individual can start walking and tens of thousands might follow … If a lion or a crocodile eats the very temporary leader, the rest barely notice, the migration continues …'

The future

The future of the migration is far from secure. Parts of the migration route are unprotected, and commercial hunting for game meat takes an estimated 40,000 animals a year, which is probably sustainable. However, Markus Borner believes that if this number were to double, wildebeest numbers would crash.

It would be sad if we are to be the last generation to witness this amazing spectacle.

Wildebeest drinking at a stream

Tarangire National Park

Tarangire is located just over 100km (62 miles) south of Arusha off a good road to Dodoma. The park occupies part of the rift valley south of Lake Manyara, and it enjoys a variety of habitats in its 1,360sq km (525sq miles), ranging from mixed savannah to low hills and extensive swampland. Dominating its ecosystem is permanent water, both in the southern swamps and along the Tarangire River. One feature, not unique, but certainly special to Tarangire is the thousands of ancient baobab trees both within and adjacent to the park.

Although part of a migration system, and therefore with variable animal numbers at different times of the year, Tarangire has some of the highest game concentrations in Africa, and is a fine place to view many species, including elephant and buffalo.

The Tarangire migration system

Tarangire does not try to compete with Serengeti. However, it is the centre of a significant annual migration system all of its own. Animals in all areas tend to disperse during rains and times of plentiful water. In Tarangire the rains

Massive baobab tree showing comparative size

(Nov–Dec) and the long rains (Apr–May). The dry periods, when animals are close to the swamps and the river are Feb–Mar and June–Oct.

The migration system involves about 3,000 elephants, more than 20,000 wildebeest and roughly 30,000 plains zebras, as well as other animals such as eland and oryx.

The Tarangire swamps

Ironically the best game-viewing areas, the swamps, have the least visitor accommodation, the poorest access and therefore the smallest number of visitors. One even needs a special permit to go south of the Kuro ranger post. However, it does mean that the extra effort to get there is almost always worth it.

Gursi Swamp, in the northwest, is most accessible, and is said to be a location for the rare and elusive African hunting dog.

Silale Swamp is next most accessible, and is a little more remote, but is great for birding, especially waterbirds.

Lamarkau and **Nguselororobi swamps** are both much more remote and are seldom visited, but will give you an experience which you do not have to share with many others. If you are an independent traveller, always take a ranger, ideally with a radio, when you visit isolated places.

Tarangire flowers

Any habitats with a seasonal rainfall regime are good places to see the wild

cause elephant, wildebeest, zebra and other large mammals to spread out, even as far as Amboseli in Kenya. In the dry season the reverse happens, and animals concentrate on the swamps. Dispersal occurs during the short rains

TSETSE FLIES

The tsetse fly causes *nagana* in cattle, which is fatal, and is why many areas of tropical Africa have no cattle. Tarangire owes its existence to tsetse flies. If they did not exist here, there would be no national park; instead it would all be cattle grazing.

In humans tsetse flies cause sleeping sickness, which is a serious disease if untreated.

Vervet monkeys and baboons are common around lodges

flowers. These tend to occur in a rapid flush during and after the same rains which cause animal dispersions. Acquire a wild flower book and double your enjoyment during this time.

Viewing elephants

Learn a little about elephants and elephant society, and you will enjoy your viewing so much more. You have the best chance of viewing elephants during the dry season, when their range is therefore more restricted. At that time you are more or less guaranteed to see elephants near rivers and permanent swamps.

During the day elephants may be widely scattered in small herds. They may spend up to 18 hours a day feeding, and it is believed that male elephants forage as far as 30km (19

Elephants pausing on their way to water

miles) from water. Mothers with calves stay much closer to water supplies.

Termite mound in Tarangire

AFRICAN ELEPHANT

Male elephants (*Loxodonta africana*) weigh over 4.5 tonnes and females 3 tonnes.

Elephants are the largest land animals. They eat over 125kg (276lb) of food a day and drink over 500 litres (110 gallons) of water. They go through six sets of teeth in their lives, and die when their teeth eventually wear out.

Elephant tusks may grow to over 100kg (220lb). They have been poached for their ivory, especially during the 1970s and 1980s, when half of them were destroyed. Numbers are presently recovering, but this depends on the continuation of the CITES ban on trade in ivory.

Tarangire National Park

An old bull elephant

On safari: the southern circuit

Southern and central Tanzania is home to some of the world's largest wildlife reserves and national parks, and some of the greatest numbers of animals. Because many of the areas are so remote and so large, the visitor experience is very different from that in the busier northern areas. There is no circuit as such, because the parks are so scattered. However, it is quite normal to visit a few parks and reserves in succession, albeit hundreds of kilometres apart. Also, unless you really want many hours of dusty driving, flying, though more expensive, is the sensible way to travel between them.

The southern circuit roughly encompasses the Rufiji River, Rufiji Delta, Selous Game Reserve and the Ruaha, Mikumi, Katavi and Udzungwa Mountains national parks.

The Rufiji River

Much of the southern safari area is in the basin of the Rufiji River and its tributaries, and it is useful to know something about the area.

This Tazara train is one way to access Selous Game Reserve

The Rufiji is Tanzania's biggest river, and it occupies about 74,000sq km (28,572sq miles) of the south-central area of the country. It has three major tributaries, the Lugwa, the Great Ruaha and the Kiolombero. Although the Ruaha has roughly half the total drainage basin area, it is the Kiolombero which supplies 65 per cent of the water.

The flow of the Rufiji (and its tributaries) is highly seasonal, and for much of the year you see a lazy, slow-flowing stream, often braided or divided, which meanders between islands of sand. Since 1990, the Great Ruaha has, on occasion, stopped flowing, and did so in 1999 for 111 days. This is thought not to be a result of weather changes like global warming, but by uncontrolled abstraction of water for rice-field and sugar-plantation irrigation.

SAFARI EXPRESS

Fox of Africa, the well-known safari company, are planning Tanzania's first private train, the Safari Express. It is designed not just as a means of transport, but as a visitor experience in itself. It will run from Dar es Salaam to Kidatu, situated between Mikumi National Park and the Udzungwa Mountains National Park, on the northern border of the Selous Game Reserve. It is planned for the train to leave Dar es Salaam on Sundays, Tuesdays and Fridays.

Male waterbuck

Explorer and hunter Frederick Courtney Selous

FREDERICK COURTNEY SELOUS

Selous gives his name to the massive Selous Reserve. He was an early 20th-century British explorer and hunter, much admired in his time, but his own personal slaughter of over 1,000 elephants was the forerunner of the massive destruction of elephants carried out by well-armed poachers in the 1970s and 80s.

Selous was killed by German soldiers in 1917 during the First World War, near the Beho Beho River, and his grave may be visited.

1992 as the Ruaha System Wildlife Management Project, and which now involves 19 experimental villages. In areas where wild animals are much more efficient at using the food resources than cattle, this may be the way forward.

The Rufiji basin has multi-purpose usage. It is the location for **Ruaha National Park**, the second-largest national park in Tanzania. It also produces 60 per cent of Tanzania's electricity, with hydroelectric power stations at Mtera, Kidatu and Lower Kihansi. In addition, the basin is one of the country's most important agricultural regions.

There are undoubtedly areas of potential conflict. One is the proposed hydro scheme at **Stiegler's Gorge**, one of the major tourist sites on the Rufiji River in the Selous Game Reserve.

One development that may surprise visitors is the existence of a sustainable game-hunting programme, started in

The Rufiji delta

The delta of the Rufiji is one of Tanzania's most important and most sensitive ecozones. It is the largest continuous mangrove forest in the world, at 5,300sq km (2,046sq miles). When it floods, the river spreads out to about 15km (9 miles) wide.

The mangroves extend 23km (14 miles) inland up the river, and there are eight common species, including *Avicennia marina* and *Ceropiops tagal*. The mangroves provide a vital environment for many life forms. Fish there include yellow fin, dogtooth, tuna, kingfish, dorado and red cod. Migratory birds such as Caspian tern, crab plover, roseate tern and little stint use the wetlands.

SELOUS GAME RESERVE

Selous is an area of superlatives. At over 50,000sq km (19,300sq miles) it is bigger than many small countries, and it is the largest wildlife reserve in Africa. Its herds of many animals are enormous – its elephant population for example, estimated at about 65,000, is bigger than the entire elephant population of Kenya. As well as boasting the largest numbers of common animals, Selous also has the largest herds of some of the rarer antelopes such as sable. Tanzania still allows limited and controlled hunting of wildlife, and Selous is divided into two, a hunting reserve in the south, and a non-hunting reserve in the north. It is dominated by the great Rufiji River which flows through the reserve,

providing the life-giving water to its animals in the dry seasons, and dominating the ecosystem and the landscape.

A word of warning is necessary after all the superlatives. Despite the enormous number of animals, and although Selous is so huge, it is not the sort of place which is 'teeming' with animals (like Katavi or Tarangire in the dry season). Even though there are 65,000 elephants, it is possible to visit and not see one.

There are no great volcanoes or a Great Rift Valley, just enormous flat plains, the quintessential Africa. Rivers are sinuous and sleepy, except in the rains when they become raging torrents. Everything in the Selous heat

On safari: the southern circuit

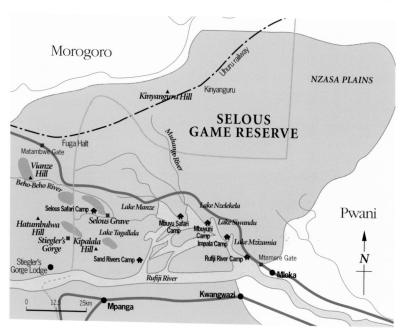

is gentle and languid. Safaris here proceed slowly, with only short morning walks and long lunches, followed by some quiet bird watching from a boat, far removed from the 'race' around the northern circuit.

The history of Selous is unique in that it has been a 'reserve' since 1905, named after the famous ('infamous' according to conservationists) Frederick Courtney Selous, who was a professional hunter for 30 years.

The highlights

In spite of earlier reservations, the highlights, apart from the sheer size of the place and that you'll probably never see another Land Cruiser, still include the huge numbers of animals (about one million large mammals are in the reserve). There are over 100,000 buffalo and about 10 per cent of the world-population of elephants. There are 3,000–4,000 lions, and many more generally unseen other cats. The reserve contains one of the biggest surviving gene pools of African wild dogs, which can be seen around the waterholes during the dry season. In addition, Lake Tagala has the world's highest density of crocodiles.

Similarly, although the landscape lacks drama, the vegetation of Selous is remarkable. There is *miombo* (deciduous woodland), an ecosystem only exceeded in biodiversity by the rainforest. There is open grassland, rocky acacia-covered hills and palm woods; there are rivers, swamps and riverine woodland, a host of different habitats and ecosystems. Moreover, the Rufiji River rises 5m (16ft) during the rains, and forms great lakes and swamps, superb for birdlife.

Selous has enormous numbers of buffalo

Inquisitive zebras at Ruaha

How to access Selous Game Reserve

You can access Selous in more ways than most parks and reserves, and can even reach it by train. The TAZARA railway runs through the reserve, and in 2004 Foxes of Africa launched their Safari Express which transports you in style to or from Dar es Salaam in about 5 hours. However most visitors arrive by air from Dar. It should be said that Selous is not the sort of place where a backpacker can just turn up, find a local bus or hitch a lift. It is a big, remote wilderness area, and that sort of facility does not exist. Also, in general, Selous is not the sort of place for the inexperienced, and possibly poorly equipped, independent traveller. Distances are enormous, and there are

virtually no repair facilities. Vehicle breakdown becomes a serious issue!

Boat safaris offer a different option. Usually these last half a day, and are based at Tagela. The river is hundreds of metres wide, and splits up into numerous braided channels and lagoons, offering superb viewing of thousands of crocodiles and hippo. Bird watching, especially of waterside species, is excellent, and of course there is the chance to see any of the mammals that need to come down to drink, especially in the dry season.

When to visit

The times to visit depend on the rains:
• The Green Season is from mid-November to mid-June when the vegetation is lush and there are few

visitors. There are more mosquitoes, and it is more difficult to see the animals.

- The Dry Season is from mid-June to mid-November. The vegetation dries out, and the animals move near to permanent water. October is the best month of all.

RUAHA NATIONAL PARK

Ruaha National Park is located in south-central Tanzania just 130km (81 miles) north of Iringa and close to the Tanzam Highway. At 10,300sq km (3,977sq miles), it is the second-largest national park after Serengeti. Mostly tourists fly in, but a good way to plan your safari by road is to move on to Ruaha after time in Selous or Mikumi; otherwise it is a long, 10-hour drive from Dar.

The park is dominated by the majestic Great Ruaha River, one of the major tributaries of the Rufiji. During the dry season, the gently meandering stream, often braided with many channels and sandy islands, is the magnet for a wide array of grazers,

Pilot checking fuel before takeoff

Young leopard at Ruaha

including the rare sable and roan antelope, together with Africa's most southerly population of Grant's gazelle. The park has both lesser and greater kudu. There are over 8,000 resident elephant, and large numbers of hippo and crocodile. As well as lion and leopard, predators include African hunting dogs, rare or locally extinct in many parks and reserves.

Ruaha is located at the meeting point of the flora and fauna of eastern and southern Africa, and so has a combination of animals and plants found almost nowhere else.

The best time to view large mammals is during the dry season, from May to December. The lower vegetation makes animal-spotting easier when they are drawn to the river to drink. Sometimes, and increasingly frequently, the river stops flowing for part of the year, and is reduced to a series of pools. Elephants dig for water with their tusks, and the possibility of seeing the full range of Ruaha's game is increased.

If you are here for the birds, then the wet season, which coincides with the time for winter migrants from the northern hemisphere, is best. The rains from January to April encourage the lush growth and the wild flowers. Birds are abundant at this time, but animals are dispersed and more difficult to see.

Ruaha has one lodge, alongside the river, and two dry-season camps. Simple self-catering *bandas* are also placed by the river, near to the park headquarters.

MIKUMI, UDZUNGWA AND KATAVI NATIONAL PARKS
Mikumi

Mikumi is part of the Selous ecosystem, and lies on the Tanzam Highway, about 4 hours' drive southwest of Dar es Salaam. The park is centred on the open grassland of the Mkata River flood plain between the Uluguru Mountains to the northeast, the Udzungwa Mountains to the southwest and Selous to the southeast.

It is the most accessible part of Selous. There is even an excellent bus service (Scandinavia) which runs from Dar es Salaam right past the park headquarters' gate, and takes about 4 hours.

Although Mikumi is accessible all year round, experience tells us that the best time to go is in the European winter, between December and March.

Mikumi has a wide range of grazers, including huge buffalo herds, zebra, giraffe, kongoni, wildebeest and a smaller form of elephant than found in other areas.

GREATER KUDU

The greater kudu (*Tragelaphus stresiceros*) (Swahili: *tondala mkubwa*) has a height of between 100 and 160cm (39–63in), and weighs about 300kg (661lbs). It is the second-largest antelope after the eland. Males have spectacular spiralling horns. Usually shy and retiring, they are found in small herds of up to about 12 animals, usually in woodland-savannah, and not too far from water. This kudu is generally rare in East Africa, but is sometimes locally common, as in Ruaha.

There are the normal predators and lions that are easy to spot in the more open grassland areas. During the months between December and March, northern migrants swell bird numbers to over 300 recorded species.

You could combine a visit to Mikumi with a trip to Udzungwa, Selous or Ruaha.

Udzungwa

Udzungwa is not for your mass tourist package tour, as it has no lodges or permanent tented camps. However, it gives you the possibility of visiting a forest landscape of primaeval beauty, of mosses, lichens, ferns and the rampant growth of the rainforest.

It is located about 60km (37 miles) south of Mikumi, and about 350km (217 miles) southwest of Dar es Salaam.

Udzungwa lacks the modern comforts which are normal in Serengeti or at Ngorongoro. However, for those who are more adventurous, it does offer the possibility of visiting an area with a precious, isolated and undisturbed genetic stock. It has six species of primates, including two endemic species, the Iringa red colobus monkey and the Sanje crested mangabe. It has many endemic birds, and is recognised as Tanzania's richest forest bird habitat.

Udzungwa is ideal for those who are fit and enjoy walking and climbing. Its centrepiece is the 170m (558ft) Sanje Waterfall.

Katavi

Katavi is Tanzania's most isolated national park, but arguably the most exciting. It will probably remain an exclusive location, as it takes several days to drive there from Arusha, or four hours of flying. The park occupies over 4,000sq km (1,544sq miles) of high, grassy flood plain, and is based around the two lakes Katavi and Chada. It is probably unmatched anywhere for its quantity and variety of animals. Even for those who are professionals in the safari business, Katavi represents the pinnacle of African adventure.

There are very few facilities. Though gazetted as a park in 1974, as recently as 2001 it had had only 84 visitors. There is only one camp, the seasonal luxury tented camp set up by Foxes of Africa, and supplied by private aircraft.

The park's lush grasslands depend on the flooding of the plains around the lakes during the rains, and their subsequent drying out during the dry season, rather like the Masai Mara Triangle in neighbouring Kenya. In the dry season, enormous numbers of animals congregate around the lakes, especially elephant, hippo and crocodile, with buffalo herds numbering in thousands. The Fox Camp is open in the dry season. The best times to go are normally May to October.

It is a destination guaranteed to provide the trip of a lifetime.

On safari: the southern circuit

Greater kudu are usually quite timid

Mount Kilimanjaro and the Usambaras

Kilimanjaro is a World Heritage Site. In 1973, the area above 2,700m (8,858ft) was designated a national park, and the zone between 1,800–2,700m (5,906–8,858ft) is a national forest park. There are six rights of way to the mountain. Most people think of the Congo when the rainforest in Africa is mentioned. However, in the eastern Usambara Mountains of northern Tanzania about 30 per cent of the primaeval forest remains, and it is now protected as part of the Tanzanian government's programme of protecting the rainforest.

KILIMANJARO

There is some confusion over the meaning of the name, ranging from 'Mountain of Light' to 'Mountain of Caravans'. In Swahili, *Kilima Njaro* literally means 'The Shining Mountain'. It is the easiest big mountain in the world to climb, and about 20,000 people attempt it each year. Financially Kilimanjaro is Tanzania's most important tourist asset, far exceeding safaris and tropical beaches in income

Close-up, Kilimanjaro icefields from Machame

Kilimanjaro showing less snow and ice on the north-facing summit

that is generated. The walk up has been likened climatically and botanically to a trek from the equator to the poles, crossing as one does first rainforest, then heath and moorland, followed by alpine desert, and finally the ice and snow, equivalent to the tundra of the high Arctic.

It is possible to do a range of activities on the mountain and in the national park. There are nature trails on the lower slopes, and you can arrange one- or two-day hikes on the Shira Plateau. However, most people come to climb the mountain, usually taking five or six days.

The best times to come are January to February and July to September. It is expensive, but in general, the more it costs, the better the equipment, which is not just a matter of comfort; it may be important to your safety (*see Directory on pp166–7*).

Climbing Kilimanjaro

Climbing Kilimanjaro is a serious business. Although you can literally walk up the mountain, because of its height, it presents real problems of altitude sickness, which can be fatal. Several climbers die on Kilimanjaro every year. So try to prepare for the climb, realise that it is not just a jaunt up the mountain, and go in a properly organised group. Of all the holidays you may ever take, this is the one for which it will pay to be prepared.

Read books like *The Mountain Club of Kenya Guide to Mt Kenya and Kilimanjaro*, edited by Iain Allan, or *Mountain Sickness* by Peter H Hackett MD, American Alpine Club.

Mount Kilimanjaro and the Usambaras

Hazards and precautions

In *The Mountain Club of Kenya Guide*, Dr Brent Blue suggests that a basic test of whether you can think of climbing Kilimanjaro is to be able to cover 8km (5 miles) in 45 minutes. If you can't, then get training. Otherwise you greatly increase the risk of having difficulties. That said, simply being super-fit is not a guarantee that you can make the ascent problem-free.

The problems are associated with the ease with which anyone can start climbing this huge and isolated mountain. Within only one hour from landing at Kilimanjaro International Airport, one can be on the mountain, compared with a week's trek to the foothills of the Himalayas. There are two main issues:

- **The cold** possibly causing hypothermia, and to a lesser extent frostbite.
- **Altitude** resulting in a series of potentially fatal conditions: hypoxia, AMS (acute mountain sickness), HAPE (high altitude pulmonary oedema) and HACE (high altitude cerebral oedema).

Hypothermia can be avoided in numerous ways. Clothing should be multi-layered to retain heat and to allow flexibility in controlling body heat and sweating as you climb. Avoid getting wet; this greatly accelerates the development of hypothermia. Protect against wind chill, especially the cooling effects of evaporation when wet. Do not sleep directly on cold ground. Wear a hat.

The effects of altitude are caused by not being properly acclimatised to the altitude, and almost everyone will have some of the symptoms. These include headache, nausea and vomiting, lack of appetite, insomnia, fatigue and dehydration. At their most extreme, these conditions are fatal and should be taken very seriously.

So what can one do to make this a happy time? The first advice is to plan the ascent over as much time as you can. Walk in, rather than drive in a vehicle. Remember that every day of acclimatisation doubles your chance of making it to the top.

If you are attempting climbs of over 3,500m (11,483ft), the Mountain Club of Kenya suggest that you take a day per extra 500m (1,640ft) ascent. Also, as much of the problem seems associated with the altitude at which you sleep, once you have made your climb, descend rapidly.

When climbers suffer from either HAPE or HACE, Peter Hackett says that

Giant groundsels – a sort of alpine mutation

there are only three treatments 'descend, descend, descend'.

In addition, there are numerous other conditions to guard against, some related to mountain climbing, others merely common sense. These include things like sunburn and snow blindness.

The above is just to make you aware that although climbing Kilimanjaro is a possibility for many people, it is also potentially highly dangerous. However, now that you have sufficient respect for the mountain, we will examine just a few of the routes.

The routes

There are three main routes, but Kilimanjaro can be climbed from most directions, albeit without the backup of fixed facilities. The recognised routes are:

- Rongai, Loitokitok and Njara from the north.
- Marangu and Maua from the southeast.
- Kidia, Umbwe and Machame from the south.
- Lemosho from the west.
- Shira from the northwest.

Whichever route you take, the ascent and descent will take 5 or 6 days. In general, the longer the trip, the more acclimatisation you will allow, and the greater your chances of reaching the Uhuru Peak summit. If you go in a small group, especially with people who know each other, you are more likely to be able to ascend and acclimatise at your own pace. Do not be too downhearted if you do not reach the summit. Using the Marangu route (the most popular tourist route),

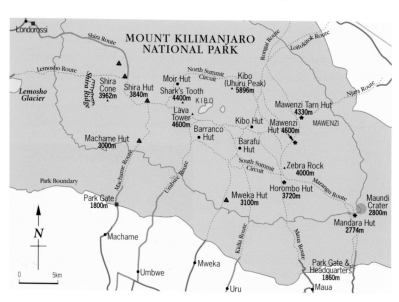

only about 20 per cent of climbers actually reach Uhuru Peak, though most do reach the crater rim. On the descent, take care as this is when most of the injuries occur.

ASCENT VIA THE MARANGU ROUTE
Day 1 – Marangu Gate to Mandara Hut
Starting at 1,860m (6,102ft) and climbing through rainforest to Mandara Hut at about 2,774m (9,101ft).

Day 2 – Mandara Hut to Horombo Hut
Climb from 2,774–3,729m (9,101–12,234ft), starting through alpine-like meadows and then moorland, with giant alpines, lobelia and groundsel.

Day 3 – Rest day at Horombo
This is your opportunity to acclimatise. The more time spent acclimatising, the more likely you are to succeed.

Day 4 – Horombo to Kibo Hut
Ascending to 4,703m (15,430ft), this is a steady climb through gravel and boulders to where one can start the final assault on the summit.

Day 5 – Kibo Hut to the summit, and descent to Horombo Hut
Typically the day starts in the middle of the night, even before midnight. To the crater rim usually takes about 6 hours, and is as far as most people get. Hopefully you are there for the sunrise over Mawenzi peak. Uhuru peak takes another 90 minutes. The descent begins immediately, initially back via Kibo, and then down to Horombo.

Day 6 – Horombo Hut to the gate
This should be a relatively relaxing walk – tired but happy – past Mandara Hut, reaching the gate by the afternoon.

MOSHI
The word *moshi* means 'smoke', and probably refers to the last eruption of Kilimanjaro about 300 years ago. Moshi is situated at the southern base of the mountain. Its economy is based on the climate produced by the world's biggest free-standing mountain, and depends very largely on coffee production.

The population of the town is about 200,000. In general, Moshi has the reputation of being more relaxed than Arusha, and the people are more laid back.

Most visitors come to the town on their way to Kilimanjaro, and will land at Kilimanjaro International Airport

'Ascent Only' notice, Machame

Glacial meltwaters of Machame River, coming from Kilimanjaro

and arrive in Moshi on an airline bus (KLM or Precision Air) or by taxi. There is no tourist office, but there is a very useful Moshi Guide, which is generally available.

The centre of the town is very compact, with everything of much importance within only about 400m (1,312ft) of the **Clock Tower**. There are few things for the tourist to see. The inevitable **'Askari Monument'**, the East African equivalent of a war memorial, is 400m (1,312ft) northwest of the clock, and the **Roman Catholic Cathedral**, the church of 'Christ the King', is next door.

The **Central Market** is about 1km (²/₃ mile) south of the Clock Tower, and has a wide range of everything, as well as being a good place for photographs.

THE USAMBARAS

As an island of endemic species, surrounded by savannah, the rainforest of the Usambara Mountains can be thought of as an African Galapagos. From about 1950 to 1986, the area around Amani was heavily logged in order to service the demand of a

sawmill in Tanga. However, in 1986 the Finnish government, for a long time the main promoters of logging, became the sponsors of conservation, with a $6.1 million grant. Logging was abandoned, and the East Usambaras Forest Project (later to become the Eastern Usambaras Conservation Programme) was established.

The programme not only stopped forest destruction, but also implemented reforestation, sustainable agriculture and education in various spheres.

Amani Nature Reserve

The Amani (meaning 'peace') Nature Reserve was designated in 1997, and has been described as 'one of Africa's largest botanical gardens'. Being off the main tourist circuits, Amani is one of the least-visited sanctuaries, but for those who yearn for the solitude of unchanged rainforest, it offers a rare experience.

Walk in the forest at Amani in the cool mountain air among giant camphor trees, strangler figs and, everywhere, liana creepers. It is a great place for birders, with over 350 species recorded. Large mammals are rare, but look up to the canopy and you will see nervous black-and-white colobus monkeys high in the treetops, looking back at you.

The forest is a superb place to see butterflies and, in comparison with national parks, you have the benefit of being out of your car so that you can get close to them.

Pawpaw (papaya)

The Usambaras have one major advantage for the visitor over other mountain forest gems such as the Udzungwa National Park – most of these mountains are quite remote, but the Usambaras at Amani are highly accessible, located just off the tarmac Arusha–Dar es Salaam road. They are half an hour's drive from the airport at Tanga, which is a mere stone's throw by air from Dar es Salaam or Zanzibar. This must become one of the star destinations of the future.

There are only two access routes to the Usumbaras. Apart from Amani the other is further west, via Lushoto. To reach Amani, leave the main Tanga to Korogwe road at Muheza, and proceed to Sigi. Pay at the Sigi Gate, and drive 9km (6 miles) on a usually well-kept murram (dirt) road to Amani itself. You can visit Amani for a day from Tanga or Pangani, or you can stay over in one of the rest houses:

• Sigi Rest House (at the gate).
• Amani Conservation Centre Rest House.
• Amani Malaria Research Centre Rest House.

Originally the Germans cleared much of the forest area around Amani for coffee plantations, though these have largely been replaced by tea estates, which are still there. There is an arboretum located in the **Amani Botanical Gardens** that has a range of the important species of the forest.

The western Usambara

The eastern and western Usambaras are separated by the valley of the Lwengera River, which is a tributary of the Pangani. The route into the western Usambara leaves the Dar es Salaam road at Mombo and heads up a paved road, following a winding river to Soni and Lushoto. **Lushoto**, which has a population of approximately 100,000, is situated at an altitude of about 1,500m (4,921ft), and has a beautiful mountain setting. It has a 'small-town' atmosphere, and the people are very friendly and welcoming. Located at a high altitude, it is much cooler than the coast, and was originally popular with the German colonists as a pleasant retreat from Dar es Salaam during the hottest months. The first European to arrive in the area was Johannes Krapf in 1849. The Germans later named the town Wilhelmstal, after the Kaiser.

The town has a busy central market, banks, a bookshop and a Tourist Information Centre. About 1km

(²/₃ mile) north of the town centre, is the Tafori Arboretum, which has a wide collection of Usambara plants. Lushoto is also host to one of Tanzania's beacon local tourist projects, the Western Usambaras Cultural Tourist Programme.

The Western Usambaras Cultural Tourist Programme is one of the foremost of such schemes in the country, and provides a wide variety of experiences for visitors, based on different aspects of local culture. It also provides an income for the local people who take part.

Information on potential tours and walks is obtained in Lushoto at the Tourist Information Centre. They offer a selection of walks, mountain climbing, visits to various development projects, visits to places where you can experience past and present local culture, and visits to view pottery-making.

Be warned that, as with most tourist sites, there are also conmen around who have nothing to do with the programme, so only take guides from the Information Centre.

Here are some samples of the trips that are available.

Rainforest

Bangala River tour

This is a lovely walk along the valley of the Bangala River, sometimes even in the river. There are beautiful views over the Maasai Plains below, and you can visit traditional Wasamba farms, a tree nursery and a primary school.
The walk takes 5 to 7 hours.

Irente Point walk

Irente is the best known of the western Usambara viewpoints. It forms a 'pulpit' rock 1,000m (3,281ft) above the surrounding plains. On the way back, the tour visits the villages of **Irente juu** and **Mwindadi**, where visitors can see various village development projects.
The trip takes 4 to 6 hours.

Tour of Usambara farm

The trip allows you to walk through the most fertile Usambara farmland, and you will visit a cheese factory on your way to the village of **Vuli**. Around the village you can see recently started projects involving soil conservation and irrigation.
The trip takes 4 to 6 hours.

Tours lasting several days

There are also cultural programmes lasting three to five days, which can be tailor-made to suit your choice. They include a **Western Usambara Mountain Tour** and a **Mazumbae Forest Reserve Tour** among others.

The trips and walks are very cheap in comparison with many other tourist activities.

Kilimanjaro, the world's largest free-standing mountain

High *shambas* just before the rainforest starts

Kilimanjaro is not only the world's largest free-standing mountain, but also one of the tallest volcanoes. The mountain is enormous, covering an area of about 80km (50 miles) by 40km (25 miles), and trending NNW to SSE.

For years it was thought that it was extinct, but today geologists believe that Kilimanjaro is only dormant and will erupt again. Fumaroles at the summit, emitting gas and liquid, are testimony to this. The Great Rift Valley, with its associated tectonic movements, is only 80km (50 miles) away, and it is believed that over millions of years Africa will tear itself apart, causing further volcanic outpourings and many earthquakes.

The present mountain is in fact made up of three major volcanoes ranging from about 1 million to 20 million years old. First was Shira in the west. Now only its southern and western crater rim remains, but before its cone collapsed it probably reached about 5,000m (16,404ft). Next came Mawenzi, in the east, still a free-standing mountain and originally reaching almost 6,000m (19,685ft). Even today it forms an impressive sight, with almost 2,000m (6,562ft) of rocky crag rising from Kilimanjaro's shoulder.

Roughly 1–2 million years ago, Kibo rose up between the two, thus forming the enormous bulk of today's mountain. It still has the classical conical volcano shape, though the summit crater is now a collapsed caldera, 2.5 km (1½ miles) wide.

All around the mountain are scores of parasitic cones and igneous intrusions, giving more evidence of this active volcanic area. To the west is active volcano Ol Doinyo Lengai, and to the north in Kenya are the Chyulu

Mountains, which belched out lava only a century ago.

Kilimanjaro glaciers

As we ascend, it gets colder by about 6.5°C (12°F) for every 1,000m (3,280ft), so at an altitude of 5,000m (16,404ft) on Kilimanjaro we can expect ice. The first European who saw the snows of Kilimanjaro was missionary Johannes Redmann in 1848, and in 1900 Hans Meyer became the first person to set foot on the glaciers at the summit.

There is also evidence in the form of old glacial moraines (deposits) that there were glaciers much lower down the mountain up to only about 12,000 years ago. During the last Ice Age (called the Pleistocene) when glaciers covered much of Europe, Asia and North America, the ice on Kilimanjaro descended to lower than 3,000m (9,843ft), and then gradually retreated back up the mountain as planetary climatic conditions changed.

At the moment, another influence on the world's weather, global warming, is causing unprecedented melting of glacier ice, and it is very sad to contemplate that at present rates there will be no glaciers on Kilimanjaro or Mount Kenya in about 10 years' time. In 1900, glaciers covered about 12sq km (5sq miles), whereas today the extent is just over 2sq km (^{3}/4sq mile). If ever we needed evidence of global warming, this must be it.

Currently the largest ice fields are the Credner (northwest summit), Northern and Ratzel (both in the crater) and the Southern ice field. As you approach Kilimanjaro from Arusha and Moshi, you will see 'ice-tongues' extending down from the summit, from west to east called Little Baranco, Great Baranco, Decken and Kersten.

Machame village, 5km (3 miles) from the Park gate

Lake Victoria and Rubondo Island National Park

Lake Victoria is the world's second-largest freshwater lake, at 68,000sq km (26,255sq miles). However, apart from exceptions such as Rubondo Island and Speke Bay, it is not a major tourist destination; Rubondo Island National Park is the one serious holiday location in Lake Victoria. There is much to be recommended. The national park was established in 1977, with an area of about 400sq km (154sq miles), of which Rubondo Island itself is just over half.

Lake Victoria

Mwanza is the gateway to the lake, and is Tanzania's second-largest city. The city is thoroughly run-down, partly because of about 1 million economic migrants who often live in appalling conditions. The roads, electricity supply and infrastructure are generally in a desperate state, and Mwanza must greatly improve before it becomes a serious tourist destination. In spite of all this, the Mwanza people are very

Rubondo Beach, Lake Victoria

welcoming to the visitor, and there is a good range of accommodation in the middle and upper price range.

Rubondo Island National Park

The national park is about 150km (93 miles) west of Mwanza, and most tourists arrive at the island directly by air from one of the international airports in East Africa. Some guests choose to come by private charter from a number of destinations. If you really feel masochistic, you can also fly to Mwanza, drive for 6 or 7 hours to Nungwe and take a boat for another hour or so to Rubondo.

Water is a major part of the landscape, and 90 per cent of the habitat is classified as 'humid forest'. However, there is also

Crocodile sunning itself on the riverbank

savannah, open woodland and papyrus swamp. Some of the flora is simply stunning, with over 40 varieties of orchid, fireball lilies and red coral trees.

The rains come mainly in November, and again from March to May, with two dry seasons, June to October, and

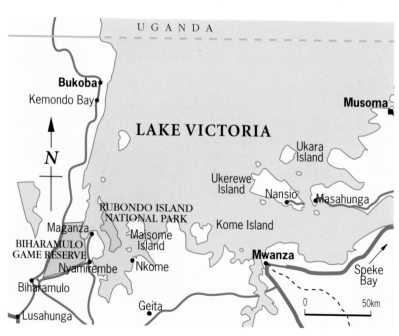

Rubondo Island Camp

December to February. The temperature is always in the range 20–26°C (68–79°F), and with the equator running through the northern end of the lake, daylight always begins between 6.30am and 7am.

Animals and birds are spectacular. The star attraction is the water antelope, the sitatunga. This is the only place in Tanzania where you will see it, and it is rare in other countries. There are many hippos, crocodiles, otters and bushbuck, together with introduced species such as elephant, chimpanzees and giraffe. There are no buffalo or rhino, and therefore walking safaris are normal and safe.

The bird watching is amazing, especially of waterbirds. Rubondo has Africa's highest density of fish eagles, together with all manner of varieties of herons, egrets, storks and kingfishers, plus almost 400 recorded species of other birds.

The best time to visit depends on what you want to do. Generally the best time is June to August; for birds it is December to February to enjoy the northern migrants; for butterflies come in November to March.

Rubondo tree hide

Rubondo is exclusive. Although there are self-catering bandas and a campsite, most visitors stay in the upmarket **Rubondo Island Camp**, which has only 10 luxury tents and offers a wide selection of activities, including chimptracking, boat trips, canoeing, fishing, walking safaris and bird watching. Or simply doing not very much from the camp's elevated site at the edge of the lake.

If you want a holiday that is exclusive, this is it.

Speke Bay

Speke Bay is located on Lake Victoria, west of the Serengeti Western Corridor, and only an hour from Kirawira or Grumeti River Camp. As well as providing something different for those on a Serengeti safari, it is also an increasingly popular stopover for those accessing the Tanzania Northern Safari Circuit from western Masai Mara, rather than via Arusha.

As with Rubondo, Speke Bay is an excellent place for bird watching, and after the sometimes dry and dusty conditions on safari, the breezy terrace of Speke Bay Hotel, overlooking the lake, can provide a lovely, refreshing experience.

Introducing the waterbirds of Lake Victoria

The range of birds is so prolific here that you might spend your entire visit just bird watching. Here are just a few common species:

African fish eagle

Unmistakeable large eagle, with its white head, tail and breast, and its gull-like call. Rubondo Island has literally hundreds of breeding pairs.

Malachite kingfisher

A stunningly beautiful bird, with a bright blue head, orange breast and red bill. A regular fisherman in the shallows around the lake.

Saddle-billed stork

At 1.45m (5ft), an uncommonly tall bird. White upper body and breast with the rest black, including its head. Distinguished by a huge black and yellow bill.

Fish eagle coming in for a catch

Lake Tanganyika, Gombe Stream and Mohale Mountains national parks

Lake Tanganyika is a truly remarkable place, with many superlatives attached to it, and for that reason is worthy of a visit. At only 52sq km (20sq miles), Gombe Stream National Park is the smallest of the national parks, but because of the work of Jane Goodall, it is one of the best known. Mahale Mountains National Park occupies over 1,600sq km (618sq miles) of dramatic, forested mountain scenery next to Lake Tanganyika.

Lake Tanganyika

Lake Tanganyika is quite exceptional in terms of its size, its age and the effects of its long-term geographical isolation. It is the longest freshwater lake in the world, occupying 677km (421 miles) of

Boy on Lake Tanganyika

the western arm of the Great Rift Valley. It is the world's second-deepest lake with a maximum depth of 1,436m (4,711ft), with its bottom 358m (1,175ft) below sea level. Moreover, whereas the lakes of Europe and North America have had a mere 10,000 years since the last Ice Age, Lake Tanganyika has been undisturbed for at least 20 million years, and with the same climate, allowing an enormously diverse flora and fauna to develop. It has over 250 endemic fish species, including over 200 cichlids.

A special way to experience the lake is on the MV *Liemba*, which has been plying the routes along the lake since the First World War. It must be one of the oldest vessels in the world still in service, having been launched originally in 1913. The boat was constructed in sections in Germany as the *Graf von Gotzen*, and was then transported to

Kigoma and reassembled during the First World War. Once the British had taken the Central Railway Line, the Germans scuttled the boat, and she stayed submerged at the mouth of the Malagarasi River from 1916 until March 1924, when she was salvaged. The vessel was then renamed after the original name for the lake, Liemba.

A journey on MV *Liemba* is an unforgettable experience, as catalogued by Michael Palin in his book *Pole to Pole*. In addition to the amazing scenery of the lake, there is the spectacle of

frenetic activity when the vessel makes its weekly stop at tiny ports such as Kalama and Mpandi around the lake.

Liemba leaves **Kigoma** on Wednesday every week for **Mpulungu** in Zambia, with numerous stops along the way, arriving on Friday. It returns to Kigoma, arriving on Sunday.

Gombe Stream National Park

Lying 25km (16 miles) south of Kigoma, it is accessed by a 1- to 2-hour chartered boat trip from Kigoma. The best time to visit may be during the rains (Feb–June and Nov–Dec), as the chimpanzees, the main object of any visit, do not seem to travel around so much then, and can be more easily located.

It is expensive to visit. Accommodation possibilities are limited, with a basic (bring your own food) hostel at Kasakela.

Inspired by palaeontologist Louis Leakey, Jane Goodall started chimpanzee research at Gombe in 1960 and stayed initially until 1975. The project continues today, and is the world's longest-running animal study in the wild.

Chimpanzees are our nearest 'cousins' in the animal world, and share about 98 per cent of our genes. Along with parallel studies at **Mahale**, Jane Goodall's research has made amazing finds, which makes us question not only the behaviour of chimps, but also our definition of humans. The following are some of the finds.

- Chimps eat an enormous range of food plants, 147 at Gombe, and an overlapping, but different range at Mahale, including some species, apparently taken purely for medicinal purposes.
- We (humans) are not the only tool-users. Among other things, chimps make and use simple tools such as twigs and grasses to extract termites from holes.
- Perhaps the most alarming discoveries were related to chimps' social behaviour. One aspect included the way in which male chimpanzees periodically patrol their group territory boundaries, often killing intruder males and even older females. Chimps have been observed indulging in various forms of cannibalism, even within their own group.
- Chimps, once thought to be entirely vegetarian, are now known to be

Cargo transfer, MV *Liemba*

omnivores, the same as humans. They are skilful, co-operative and highly successful hunters, and eat a range of monkeys, especially red colobus, together with other animals such as bushpigs.

Before visiting Gombe, you will find reading at least one of Jane Goodall's books will greatly enhance your experience. Also refer to the website *www.janegoodall.org*

Mahale Mountains National Park

This park is also sometimes called **Ngungwe**, after its main peak at 2,460m (8,071ft) above sea level. Mahale is home to nine different primate species and over 1,000 chimpanzees, which have been studied since 1965 by Japanese primate researcher Junichiro Itani.

Shore near Kigoma

It is also a good place for birds and butterflies. Also, although Mahale is best known for its chimpanzees, the national park has a wide range of other animals, including lion, buffalo, eland, greater kudu, together with the rare sable and roan antelopes. If you are lucky, you can even see African hunting dogs.

It is not easy to get there, and therefore the park will remain a fairly exclusive destination. The normal route is by air from Arusha, and then by charter boat (7 hours) from Kigoma, followed by a further 1 to 2 hours in a small local boat – visiting Mahale is not a casual experience!

Once you are there, the only way of getting around is to walk. So, to visit Mahale, you must be reasonably fit; otherwise you might have a fairly unhappy experience.

Your visit normally centres round chimp-watching, which involves a fairly physical trek to locate where the animals spent the previous night and where they are now. There are more than 15 chimp communities, and their territories extend beyond the national park boundaries. Visitors will most likely track the Minikire group.

Though Gombe is more accessible, Mahale has better accommodation, throughout the range.

The best time to visit is during the dry seasons, especially between May and October. The park fees are cheaper than Gombe, but still high relative to other parks.

Guidelines for watching chimpanzees

Viewing all animals in the wild should always be done sensitively. However, the survival of chimpanzees in the wild is far from certain, and is indeed precarious. So the following are a few rules on how to have your experience

Boat on beach at Mahale

Lake Tanganyika, Gombe Stream and Mohale Mountains national parks

without over-intruding into their environment.

- Do not approach too close to chimps, and never closer than 5m (16ft), preferably 10m (33ft).
- If chimps come near you, do not engage with them. Behave like you are ignoring them.
- Do not visit at all if you have an infectious disease, like a cold or flu. Chimps are susceptible to most human illnesses.
- Never feed the animals.
- Be quiet; best not to talk at all.
- Avoid eye contact.
- Do not pursue chimps that want nothing to do with you.
- Sit down rather than stand.
- Do not take flash photographs. Best use a long lens and fast film.

Sunset at Mahale

CHIMP-WATCHING

It is sad that, after more than four decades, Jane Goodall's chimpanzee project now receives considerable criticism. It appears that 'human habituated' chimpanzees become much more aggressive, exhibiting more extremely violent behaviour than populations which do not live in such close contact with people. This raises questions over whether the sort of study Jane Goodall has conducted has a long-term and continuing viability. It also asks the question whether tourism, based on this sort of project, is in the interests of the animals.

Your guide will advise you on other details, especially if a chimpanzee becomes aggressive.

Kigoma

Kigoma is the capital of Western Province, and is important as it is the western end of the central railway line. Tourists go there en route to either Gombe or Mahale, or to catch the MV *Liemba*, the world's oldest still-functioning passenger ship.

Kigoma was originally a German trading base, and with the completion of the railway in 1914, and the arrival of the prefabricated sections of the MV *Liemba*, the German colonists felt it had a great future. However, within a year the British had taken over and *Liemba* was beneath the waters of Lake Tanganyika. But Kaiser House is still the seat of government today, and after salvage from the lake, MV *Liemba* has now completed over 4,000 trips, of about 1,000km (621 miles) each, around the lake.

Kigoma is a very modest town, centred on the wide square in front of the railway station, with a single main street, not much more. It has a sleepy, laid-back atmosphere, far removed from the normal tourist 'honey-pots', and you can walk around without being continually pestered. There are plenty of local shops, a fish market selling fresh produce from the lake, and a most incongruous 60,000-seat football stadium.

Nearby is **Ujiji**, formerly a slave trading port, and famous for the meeting of Stanley and Livingstone.

The infamous Tippu Tip from Zanzibar used Ujiji as his ferry port, linking with the Congo. A line of mango trees still marks the start of the long caravan route back to Bagamoyo and Zanzibar.

Ujiji today is a sleepy backwater, witness to the fact that slaves from here went not to the USA, but to the Indian Ocean and the Gulf. Otherwise it might have become a major tourist 'Mecca'. You can still see the Arabic influence, in the wearing of *kangas* and *kikoys*.

There is a small, nondescript memorial to Livingstone and Stanley's meeting.

Chimpanzee, Mahale

Lake Tanganyika, Gombe Stream and Mahale Mountains national parks

Lake Nyasa

Lake Nyasa is not one of Tanzania's great tourist destinations, but it is important to mention it because it is, in many ways, one of the world's most fascinating destinations. Presently most visitors are backpackers and hikers, but the area will, no doubt, cater for other more adventurous tourists from other groups in future.

Sadly, the area's history is interwoven with the slave trade. During the 18th and 19th centuries, Omani slavers raided the lake area and took slaves to the Indian Ocean ports of Kilwa and Lindi for transport to the slave markets in Zanzibar.

The name *nyasa* means 'great water' or simply 'lake' in Yao. Lake Nyasa is the third-biggest lake in Africa. It is 560km (348 miles) long and only 75km (47 miles) wide at its narrowest. However, it is 706m (2,316ft) at its deepest near **Nkhata Bay**, and its average depth is almost 300m (984ft). In comparison with Lake Tanganyika, it is made up of only one great basin, although the deepest parts are at the northern end of the lake. Indeed, in some places in the north the lake bed shelves very rapidly from the shore into water over 200m (656ft) deep.

Among the well travelled, Lake Nyasa is regarded as one of the most beautiful lakes in Africa. It is a product of the faulting system which starts in Lebanon, runs down through the Red Sea, then East Africa, and eventually out to sea near the mouth of the Zambezi.

Being between 9 and 14 degrees south of the equator, the lake tends to have more obvious seasons than other parts of Tanzania, and it is best to visit between September and November, or between June and August when it is drier and the humidity at its lowest.

The most amazing thing about Lake Nyasa is its ecosystem. As with Lake Tanganyika, Lake Nyasa has been isolated from other ecosystems for many millions of years, giving the lake the greatest freshwater biodiversity in the world. The result has been the proliferation of species, most notable being the cichlid, a small lake fish. Almost 400 species have been named, with others still being discovered, and of all species identified, so far only six are not endemic to the lake. If you wish to find out more, check the website *http://malawicichlids.com*

When you do travel to Lake Nyasa, the first thing you will discover is that it is isolated, and on the Tanzanian side a long way from almost anywhere. **Matema** is a nice place in which to do not very much. It has beautiful beaches, very clear water – average surface temperature 28°C (82°F) – and mountains nearby, together with interesting caves, waterfalls and wildlife, especially hippos and crocodiles.

There are two places to stay, the **Lutheran Beach Resort** and the **Matema Eco-tourism Resort**. Both are fairly basic, but the latter is newer, has mosquito nets (important) and offers cheap, passable meals.

Ferries on Lake Nyasa

Along with much of the infrastructure of Africa, the lake ferries have suffered, and there has been little recent investment. However, there are two ferries that operate in the Tanzania sector, the MV *Songea* and the MV *Ilala*. The main Tanzania port is **Itungi Port**, not so much a port, but the point at which small boats ferry you out into

HIRE A DUGOUT CANOE

There are not many places in the world where hiring a dugout canoe would be a normal transport option. However, one such place is on Lake Nyasa. At Matema you can hire a dugout to visit Lyulio market, at the mouth of the Lufilyo River, to watch crocodiles, hippo and birds. Also you can go to the Friday Market at Ikombe to buy the lovely cream-and ochre-coloured pottery made by Kisi women.

Lake Nyasa

the lake to access the ferry. Lack of dredging has allowed the harbour to silt up, and the boats can no longer go alongside.

MV *Songea* leaves port about midday on Thursday for **Mbamba Bay**, the last port in Tanzania, and takes about 24 hours. The boat has a 'first-class' section with some bunks, and the journey is described in one well-known guide as 'one of Africa's great journeys'. At the little harbours and villages along the way, the boat is met by flotillas of dugouts, mainly plied by women and children, selling food.

A journey for the more adventurous traveller, but one which is certainly guaranteed to be memorable.

Dugout boats come alongside the ferries

The Swahili culture of the coast

Nothing is more revealing about the history of a country or a region than the words that have been assimilated into its language. The traditional language of the coast of Tanzania, and now official language of the country, is Kiswahili, meaning in Arabic 'the language of the sailors' (literally 'the sail'). The language and culture of Tanzania's coast and the islands is a veritable mixture of the influences of the mainland of Africa, modified by all those who have chosen to raid or trade with the area during the centuries. Also we see it not only in language, but in religion, dress, food and architecture. There is a truly 'Swahili' culture, which makes the coast and the islands a special place to visit.

Early trade

It is part of Swahili legend that the King (or Sultan) of Shiraz in Persia (present-day Iran), arrived at Zanzibar in AD 975. So began a trade between the Persian Gulf, the Indian subcontinent and the coast of East Africa which was to thrive until the arrival of the Portuguese in 1498. By the 14th century, Mombasa, Kilwa and Zanzibar were all powerful trading cities. Ships sailed south with the northeast monsoon during the northern winter, and returned to India or the Gulf in the northern summer on the southwest monsoon winds. Then for 200 years the Portuguese were in control, eventually being defeated by Oman in 1698. Two hundred years on saw the arrival of the Germans and eventually, before independence, the British.

Early trade was in gold and ivory, then later in slaves, tortoiseshell, leopard skins and rhino horn. Every trading group brought something to this cultural melting pot along the coast of Africa.

Ornate Swahili door, Bagamoyo

A *kanga* used as headdress

The cultural mix
Language

Out of all this came Kiswahili, a hybrid of Bantu languages, Persian, Arabic and Hindi, with Portuguese, German and English all thrown in for good measure. Arabic speakers will recognise the similarity between many Kiswahili words and Arabic. Often in Kiswahili the only difference is an extra 'u', 'a' or 'i' on the end of the word. Kiswahili is now spoken by 95 per cent of the population.

Islam

A thousand years ago Islam came to East Africa, and the oldest surviving building in Zanzibar is the Kizimkazi Mosque, dating from AD 1107. Islam affects everything along the coast – the religion, the dress of both men and women, and the architecture of, and designs on, buildings. There is no doubt that one is in a Muslim society, but that it is uniquely East African.

Houses have traditional doors, often decorated with Koranic inscriptions. Often they have a shaded courtyard, typical of many other Muslim cultures. Some are fortified. There is even a tradition in ornate furniture, which is very much of the coastal culture.

The food

Finally, the food is different. Gone is the *ugali* (maize) and beans, to be replaced by fish, shellfish and rice, with the influence of India being evident in the use of spices, which one does not find in traditional food inland.

Dar es Salaam

The majority of tourists in Tanzania never see Dar es Salaam, most arriving as they do for holidays either on the Northern Safari Circuit or at Zanzibar. It is a pity, as Dar has much to offer. Dar is a large and rapidly expanding city (4 million people), with a population growth rate perhaps as high as 10 per cent per annum. However, those who do come here find a much more laid-back place than many other cities in Africa, and the people are seen as gentle and friendly.

Hotels on the coast

Hotels at the coast vary from the large ones with several hundred beds, following a nondescript international format, to something more individual and more culturally sensitive. The big hotels are usually centred round a pool, the open-air bars and restaurants.

Rooms everywhere will normally face the sea, and all those in the middle and upper range will have en-suite facilities.

A spacious and airy room at The Palms

Fans and air conditioning are normal in large hotels.

However, it is possible that your experience of 'paradise' even in upmarket resorts, will come with no air conditioning or fans, which can be quite stifling if you also have to use a mosquito net. It is worth checking on this.

Often rooms will have a *makuti* (thatched) roof. Frequently they are spacious, and will also include a sitting/lounging area out on the verandah, allowing you to look out on the lagoon and the reef. Many have a hammock. Furniture is normally traditional, carved Zanzibar or Swahili style.

Public areas are usually open to sea breezes, which can be quite refreshing when the humidity is high.

Alcohol is generally available even though this is a predominantly Muslim area; however, there are exceptions. Check, if you like a bottle of wine. Food is generally good, and can be excellent.

View across Dar es Salaam harbour

Often the hotels are the best places to eat in town.

In Dar, some of the best hotels, such as Mövenpick Royal Palm and Holiday Inn, are not on the beach but occupy multistorey blocks as in most big cities. Though standards are very good, you would not know where in the world you were if you suddenly woke up in one of their standard hotel rooms.

Oasis in the city – Holiday Inn, Dar es Salaam

Tingatinga painters at work

History

We can think of Dar as being a melting pot, similar to other world cities which have been formed from many influences. Here, the input of Africans, Arabs, Asians and lastly Europeans can all be seen in the various aspects of culture. But until the mid-1860s, Dar was little more than a fishing village, albeit on an inlet with enormous potential for a harbour. **Bagamoyo**, just a little up the coast, had been the mainland terminus for the slave trade, and of much more interest to the ruling Omanis.

In the 1860s, Dar was located near present-day State House. In 1886, Sultan Majid built his 'House of Peace' here, and the next year the German East Africa Company established a trading station. In 1891, as a result of having a vastly superior natural and more sheltered harbour than Bagamoyo, Dar es Salaam became the capital.

By 1894, the Germans started planning the railway, which was to eventually reach **Kigoma** in 1914.

Under firstly the Germans and then the British from 1916, Dar es Salaam's modern structure was developed. Initially the city plan and use of the land had an undoubtedly racial theme. There were areas that were definitely European (Usunguni), Asian (Uhindi) and African (Uswahilini), and to some extent these are still visible today.

In many ways the city epitomises what is going on in the country, and throughout Africa, with modern glass tower blocks next to urban slums, and shiny limousines hooting to overtake handcarts pushed by bare-footed boys.

What to see in Dar es Salaam

It is worth saying that although Dar is generally believed to be safer than most African cities, because of the enormous disparity in levels of wealth in the city and between the poor people and the tourist, some crime is inevitable. Take care, or avoid the following areas, especially at night: Bibi Tit Mahamed Street, Kariakoo, Magomeni, Ocean Road, the beach and the bus station.

Be sensible: leave valuables in the hotel safe; do not obviously flaunt your wealth; leave the Rolex and the jewellery at home. If you are unfortunate enough to be mugged, just give them everything.

A good way to get around in Dar is to hire a taxi by the hour (the price may be negotiable). Apart from his local knowledge, your taxi driver is also handy to have around in certain areas.

Central Dar

Samora Avenue is the focus for shopping in downtown Dar, and many of the important offices and banks etc. are in that general area. As well as the shops, the streets are lined with little kiosks or *dukas*, which sell almost anything. At the junction of Samora Avenue and Azikiwe Street is the **Askari Monument**, the city's most famous statue, built to commemorate the African dead, of both sides, in the First World War.

Ocean Road is the location for Dar's two most imposing relics of colonial architecture, the two major cathedrals – **St Joseph's Cathedral**, built in 1897, and the **Azania Front Lutheran Church**, started a year later. Both are good places to go if you enjoy lively Christian worship.

The **Ocean Road Cancer Hospital** has an interesting history. It was originally the **German Malaria Research Laboratory** and the workplace of Richard Koch, Nobel Prize winner, whose ultimate claim to fame was as the discoverer of the vectors of both bubonic plague and sleeping sickness.

The area between State House and the fish market was the first location of the fishing community that was the origin of Dar, and it is still a place of boats. It is a pity it is off-limits for photographers, as the present mixture of boat-building, broken boats from the past and the paraphernalia of fishing makes for superb pictures.

The **Fish Market** is located 200m (220yds) north of Kivukoni Ferry. Although you are unlikely to buy anything there, it is an education in terms of a whole new variety of fish on sale, from barracuda to squid, and from red snapper to a range of

Quiet afternoon in Samora Avenue, downtown Dar

shellfish. Take pictures, but remember to ask first.

At the **Shell Market**, across the road, you can see the most beautiful array of all kinds of shells and coral. But beware – export of shells from Tanzania is illegal, and many varieties are subject to the worldwide CITES ban on endangered species (*see box below*). The general advice is that, attractive as they are, shells for sale represent an unacceptable threat to the marine environment.

Shells for sale

SHELLS – TO BUY OR NOT TO BUY

Shells are undoubtedly beautiful, and have been bought as souvenirs by tourists for decades. Everywhere along the coast there are stalls selling them. However, this is one of the areas where tourism can be immensely destructive, and where buying shells is contributing to their ultimate destruction. The same applies to coral, which is protected by CITES, the international agreement covering trade in endangered species.

So, the advice is that however lovely shells are, avoid the temptation to buy them. Leave them in the sea where they belong.

The **National Museum** is small and dusty, but worth a visit. There is a small entrance fee, and you also have to pay if you wish to take pictures. There are several halls, including the Hall of Man (human evolution, especially Oldupai – formerly Olduvai), the Marine Biology Hall and the Ethnography Room, which gives you an insight into a small selection of tribal history.

The **Village Museum**, in Kijitonyama on New Bagamoyo Road, is worthwhile. Started in 1966, the year before Julius Nyerere set about destroying traditional village culture, ultimately without success, the museum set out to record 16 tribal housing styles, with replica buildings and their contents.

Nyumba ya Sanaa (the House of Art) is well worth a visit. It is located next to the Royal Palm Hotel on Upanga Street, and is the workplace and display gallery for hundreds of artists. The quality is generally very high, and art forms include jewellery, textiles, ceramics, Makonde carvings and Tingatinga paintings among others.

Oyster Bay (Coco Beach) and **Msasani Peninsula**, on the coast north of the city, are especially popular with the locals, particularly Asians. At the weekend, when the northeast *kaskazi* wind is blowing from the sea, hundreds drive out along the Oyster Bay road to park by the beach and cool down in the sea breeze. An industry of small stalls and *dukas*, selling *nyama choma* (barbecued meat) and curries, caters for the crowds.

The affluent face of Tanzania in downtown Dar

The **Tingatinga Art Centre** is in Selassie Street on the Msasani Peninsula, and is probably the place to buy your Tingatinga paintings. There is a huge selection, with keen pricing, and many are painted on canvas and can be rolled up for easy transport. Others done on hardboard will fit flat in your luggage. You can see the artists working, and they are very friendly and interested in chatting. Tingatinga's son, David, is one of the artists working there.

The **Slipway** is the major waterfront development, located on the west side of the Msasani Peninsula, and comprises shops, cafés, a good bookshop and a lively weekend market.

The **Zanzibar Ferry** leaves from the southern end of Ocean Road. If you must take the ferry, and many find it an interesting and different experience from flying, take someone with you when buying your tickets (a taxi driver or someone from your hotel). More than anywhere, the ferry terminal appears to be a hotspot for touts and conmen, all trying to make a buck at your expense. It is also very easy to be parted from your baggage here – best travel light and carry it yourself.

Kariakoo

Kariakoo was the original African quarter of the town, and is still quite definitely the place where the rest of Tanzania visits when they come to Dar es Salaam. Kariakoo is the area west of the city centre beyond Mnazi Mmoja Park. Here is a very traditional way of life where people live, and make and sell things, rather like a high-density African village in the city. It is not ostensibly a tourist area, and if you visit, you may be the only tourists around at the time. However, it will give you a different insight from the tree-lined boulevards of downtown Dar. The centre of Kariakoo is a large, covered market in which you can buy most things, but especially exotic foodstuffs and spices. You may find yourself an object of fascination just as strange as the lifestyle you, yourself, are viewing. Remember to ask before taking photographs.

Railway stations
There are two railway stations.
The station for the old, central line is about 400m (1,312ft) beyond the ferry terminal on Ocean Road, and looks a sorry sight, as it is one of the major victims of the post-colonial decline in infrastructure. Carriages lie disintegrating as if abandoned.

The **Tazara** station is out of town. The station building is similar to many around the world in that it seems like a monument to industrial achievement, a sort of transport palace rather than the functional building where you simply buy your ticket and wait for the train. Tazara trains are enormously long, about 20 carriages, pulled by an engine that hardly seems big enough to move such a massive train.

What to do, where to eat
Dar has loads of places to eat. At the top of the range are the often excellent hotel restaurants, such as the Serengeti in Royal Palm Hotel. In the middle range, there are many reasonably priced restaurants of almost all international cuisines: Italian, Japanese, Indian, Chinese, Ethiopian, Irish and Malaysian to name a few. At the bottom end, there are numerous small cafés and plenty of street food.

Oyster Bay, Dar es Salaam

Inevitably, standards of hygiene deteriorate as you go down the scale (*see also Food and Drink on pp168–9*).

There is only one proper cinema, the Avala, but there are lots of clubs and entertainment.

Sport and games
Dar is not the greatest place in the world for sport, but you may be surprised as you look out of your window at Holiday Inn or Royal Palm to see the influence of the British still there, with a cricket pitch, still used at weekends. Also, there is a rather poorly maintained golf course, and some excellent tennis courts. For the young at heart needing water for their sport, **Wet and Wild** is located at the southern end of Kunduchi Beach, and boasts the biggest water park in East Africa, with 22 water chutes, together with many other ways of amusing children, such as pool tables and go-karts.

The beaches
North of Dar

The main developed beaches are north of Dar, particularly Jangwani, Kunduchi and Bahari. Developments include well-equipped and relatively expensive hotels. They all offer the basic beach-hotel formula: sun, sea and pool.

Outside the hotel compounds, security is a recent problem, and guests are recommended to stay within hotel or resort grounds.

Jangwani is located along the Bagamoyo road, and is the most developed of the northern beaches, with a good reef and scuba diving. **Waterworld** has four pools, slides and other activities such as paddleboats. Food is available only in the hotels and at Waterworld.

Kunduchi and Bahari

These are located slightly further towards Bagamoyo, with the added attraction of a small fishing village and the Kunduchi Ruins. The beach is similar to Jagwani, but less developed.

Kunduchi Ruins are of an old Swahili town, including a 16th-century mosque. Not a lot is known about the town, except that it was part of the extensive trading network along the East African coast during medieval times.

Located at the southern end of Kunduchi Beach is Wet and Wild, East Africa's biggest water park, with a 1,000sq m (10,764sq ft) pool and 22 water slides.

Again, watch out for muggers outside resort compounds.

South of Dar

The southern beaches are accessed via the Kivukoni Ferry, near the fish market. Generally they are not developed, have few places to stay, and have few tourists and few muggers. If you want to get away from it all for a day, this could be the place.

Mikadi and **Mjimwene** beaches are the nearest.

Wet and Wild at Kunduchi Beach

Walk: Ocean Road

It is a fact that most expatriates living in Dar es Salaam do not walk very much, and simply being on a walk marks you out as a tourist. Though reputedly safer than many African capitals, the city is full of beggars and street children, and you will be hassled. Leave all your valuables, money, traveller's cheques, credit cards and passport in the hotel safe. If you are mugged, don't resist; just give them everything.

Dar can be very hot at times, so start your walk in the cool of the day, and finish in the shade of the Botanical Gardens or in the coffee shop of the Holiday Inn.

1 Zanzibar Ferry Terminal
The start of the walk, at the west end of Ocean Road, opposite the cathedral.

2 St Joseph's Roman Catholic Cathedral
This is one of the city's main landmarks. Stay on the cathedral side of the road, otherwise you will be pestered by all those who hang out at the ferry.

3 Azania Front Lutheran Church
St Joseph's and this Lutheran church about 200 metres (220yds) further east, were both completed a century ago and are great places to go if you want to experience lively Christian worship. Some criticise their architecture as being more suitable for parts of Europe, but it is difficult to define what

sort of large church fits in best in a mainly Muslim country.

Beyond the Azania Front Church, the next buildings are mostly former British colonial offices, which are now used as government buildings. So now cross the street for harbour views.

4 The Harbour
What you see is an absolute maritime hotchpotch of ancient-looking *dhows* and fishing boats, modern container ships, ferries and a large number of rusting hulks. Across the bay is the modern port, and to your right are the ferries to Zanzibar and the islands.

5 Kigamboni Ferry
To your left is the blue 'roll-on, roll-off' ferry that takes pedestrians and cars across to the peninsula and south coast.

6 New Kivukoni Fish Market
This market is worth a visit, just to see the amazing and unusual fish that make up the catch. It is a good place for

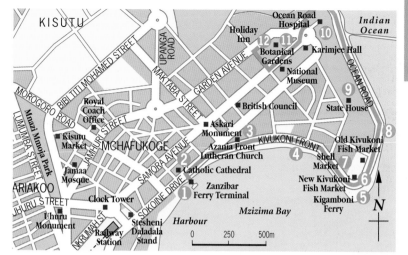

photographs, but remember to ask first. Some will refuse, but most people are happy to oblige.

7 Shell Market

Across the road is the Shell Market, which presents one with a dilemma. The range of shells is truly beautiful, but many are endangered species, and it is illegal to take them home. The best-informed opinion tells us not to buy or encourage the trade in shells.

8 Old Kivukoni Fish Market

Back on the other side of the road, north of the Fish Market, is a truly fascinating area, mainly devoted to boats and fishing. There are dugouts being made, and boats hauled up and rusting away. There are nets laid out for repair and drying, and there are sails being made and sails being fitted. This is strictly a no-photograph zone, as the State House is just up the road.

9 State House

This is the home of the president. Everyone gets to photograph Buckingham Palace or the White House, but African presidents are obviously too coy about where and how they live.

10 Ocean Road Cancer Hospital

The last building we pass on Ocean Road is the Cancer Hospital, hardly a tourist attraction, but it has historical interest as the German Malaria Research Laboratory before 1916. Past the hospital, turn left into Chimara Road, and then into Garden Avenue.

11 Botanical Gardens

You can rest and enjoy the shade of these beautiful gardens.

12 Holiday Inn

Other tourists may prefer to rest and have a cool drink at the Holiday Inn.

The *dhow*

Dhow repair at Marahubi

For several thousand years not only was the *dhow* the vehicle of trade in the Indian Ocean, but its construction was the region's most important manufacturing industry.

The *dhow* trade

Until late in the 20th century, *dhows* relied on the wind, specifically the alternating 'monsoon' of the northwest Indian Ocean. In the northern winter, between January and April, traders from the Gulf, from Muscat, Basrah and Kuwait, would arrive off the coast of East Africa blown by the 'northeast monsoon', calling at Mogadishu, Kismayu, Lamu and eventually Zanzibar. They returned during the latter part of the year on the 'southwest monsoon'.

They brought with them traditional Arabic chests (richly carved and studded with brass), carpets from Persia, and spices, dates, salt, ornate copper trays and curved daggers from Muscat. On the return voyage, they took mangrove poles, ivory, exotic fruits and, for many centuries, African slaves.

Life on board was hard. The crew slept on deck and observed Muslim prayer times. Women passengers stayed permanently below deck.

Dhow loaded with charcoal, Shangani Point

Portuguese in the Indian Ocean in the early 16th century. The early *dhow* shape with a graceful double-pointed end began to be replaced with square-ended vessels.

Dhows carry a characteristic triangular 'lateen' sail. Also, in the times before modern navigation methods, they carried a device known as the '*karmal*', which allowed them to measure latitude by gauging the height of the Pole Star above the horizon.

Once the *dhows* had discharged their cargo, they could not return home until the monsoon turned around, which might be several months if they had arrived early. The vessels were cleaned during their stay in Zanzibar, and the underwater timbers scrubbed. They were repaired if necessary, and a layer of lime and beef fat was applied to the hull. Fish oil was used to treat the deck timbers.

What is a *dhow*?

The *dhow* was the most graceful of sailing vessels. There were many different forms, and *dhow* construction went through a variety of phases. Earliest *dhows* were simple dugouts with teak planks on their sides to form a hull. Early *dhows* did not use nails, but were 'sewn' together using coconut fibre. Nails appeared in construction, and designs changed, with the arrival of the

The names of *dhows*

Dhows were named according to their shape, size and decoration. They could carry from only two or three people up to about seventy. The *ghanjah* was a large vessel, with a curved bow and a highly ornate and decorated transom at the stern. The *baghlah* was similar to a European galleon, whereas double-ended *dhows* like the *boom* have both stem- and sternposts. The *badan* was a small vessel with a shallow draught. The *ngalawa* is a small dugout fishing boat with the traditional *dhow* lateen sail.

Today, although there is still *dhow*-building in the Gulf states mainly as an attempt to allow the tradition to survive, along the Tanzanian coast *dhows* are becoming relegated to history. However, it is still possible to take a *dhow* trip and savour something of a tradition so vital to the Swahili coast.

The northern coast:
Bagamoyo, Tanga and Pangani

It takes about an hour to drive the 70km (43 miles) on a superb new road from Dar es Salaam to the ruins of Bagamoyo. At the edge of the town the tarmac ends abruptly, and one is decanted into the potholed murram (dirt) road, where you will find Bagamoyo. Tanga is situated on the coast about 200km (124 miles) north of Dar, about 35km (22 miles) if you travel by road. Pangani is located 50km (31 miles) south of Tanga, on a murram road, at the mouth of Tanzania's second-longest river, the Pangani.

BAGAMOYO

During most of history, Bagamoyo has been far more important than Dar, but during the last century it became a set of decaying ruins. The town was originally the mainland terminus for the slave routes that led from Lake Tanganyika, before it became the capital of German East Africa.

In Swahili, *bagamoyo* means 'lay down your heart'. It was here that those slaves who survived the three- to six-month walk from the interior, usually carrying ivory, eventually gave up all hope of freedom and of returning to their people. Over one million slaves in total were processed through Bagamoyo to the slave markets of Zanzibar. At the

Ruins ready for restoration, Bagamoyo

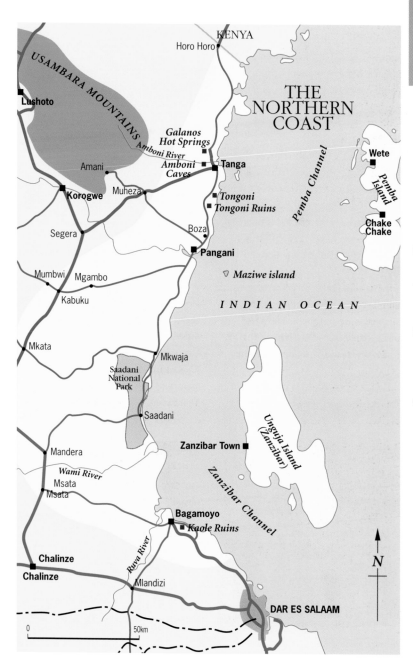

height of the trade, perhaps up to 50,000 slaves passed through in a single year. Once sold, they might end up anywhere in the Indian Ocean – India, Arabia or in the clove plantations of Zanzibar and Pemba.

What to see

Bagamoyo is a vast collection of deteriorating ruins, which desperately need the sort of restoration that has now begun in some parts of Zanzibar's Stone Town. Perhaps there is an attitude that questions the preservation of the material evidence of such an awful trade.

Most sites are close to the waterfront, and there are official guides who will show you around them. The sites include the **Arabic Tea House**, the **Customs House**, the **German Boma**

Present Catholic Mission Church, Bagamoyo

and the **Old German Fort**, built in 1897. However, do be careful as the Customs House especially is presently quite unsafe, and there is a fair amount of loose masonry and rubble.

One amusing exhibit is the doorway at the Anglican church, with the sign 'Through this door, David Livingstone passed', with the explanation that the door frame had been transported hundreds of kilometres from its original site on Lake Tanganyika to its present location.

Slavery eventually ended officially in 1873, although it continued illegally for many more years.

Much of the credit must go to the Holy Ghost Fathers, who from 1868 began buying slaves, mainly children, in order to give them their freedom. They housed them in what they called **Freedom Village** at the north end of the town, and by 1872 there were over 300 freed slaves.

Today at the site of Freedom Village there is a church, dating from 1872, and also a museum that catalogues the story of the mission and its fight to have slavery outlawed.
Open: 10am–5pm.

Souvenirs for tourists in Bagamoyo are relatively low-key. However, there is one site that is definitely worth supporting. Near the end of the tarmac, just off the road, is a project designed to help women craft-workers and entrepreneurs, called Bagamoyo Living Art and Handicraft Design Centre. Established in 1966, it trains women to increase their own commercial viability by helping them develop a variety of skills. Their work includes pottery, textiles and basketry. One can watch the women at work, and there is a small display area with goods for sale.

TANGA

Tanga is a sizeable town (about 200,000), though you would not think it from its level of services. It is situated on the south side of a large, natural harbour at a place on the coast where the fresh water and silt from the Amboni River cause a break in the coral reef. The airport is a few kilometres west of the town. The port is the second busiest in Tanzania, but has a general air of being run-down and underused, reflecting the decline of Tanga's economy as the sisal business has contracted over the last half-century.

Tanga history

The oldest remaining evidence of early settlement is from 14th-century Shirazi ruins and graves on **Toten Island**, located in the middle of the harbour.

Harvesting seaweed near Tanga

There is little to show that the Portuguese lived here, but the Omanis, who ruled the coast after 1698, certainly used Tanga as an export route for both slaves and ivory.

The Germans occupied Tanga from 1888 until 1917, and their biggest contribution was the introduction of sisal, traditionally Tanzania's main export crop. The British ruled Tanga from 1917 until independence, and initially there was a general expectation that the port would grow to rival Mombasa and Dar es Salaam. However, the invention of synthetic fibres in the middle of the last century put paid to that. Although sisal is still grown and exported, the last 50 years have seen a general decline in Tanga's economic fortunes.

There is as yet no serious tourist industry, and no top-class hotels. Most of the tourist-related services are the run-down remnants of a former colonial and expatriate society, such as the Sailing Club and the Golf Club. However, the town and its surrounding area do have their merits, and provide a destination much less commercial than the more popular safari and beach circuits.

In and around Tanga

The **Amboni Caves** are situated a few kilometres north of Tanga on the Amboni River, and are the biggest limestone cave complex in East Africa. They are largely unexplored, and represent an important tourist attraction for the future. For the casual tourist, the caves display the normal range of stalactites, stalagmites and the like. Perhaps inevitably in Africa, the guide comes with a range of stories of the caves extending all the way to Mombasa, or alternatively to Kilimanjaro.

The Tongoni ruins

The ruins are situated about 20km (12 miles) south, just off the Pangani road, and represent the deserted remains of a 14th- and 15th-century Shirazi town, and about 40 tombs. They are the largest collection of Shirazi graves in East Africa. It is clear that the town continued during the Portuguese era (1498–1698), and then became deserted some time after the 17th century. One can see the remains of a mosque, and archaeologists have found evidence of trading links between the town and Persia. It is also possible to

Seaweed drying

see more recent evidence of a sort of 18th- and 19th-century 'renaissance', when former residents of Kilwa moved north and occupied the site, but only for a time.

Seaweed farming

Visit villages on the east coast of Unguja, and most days you can see hundreds of folk working in the lagoon, between the shore and the fringing reef. Are they fishing? No, they are farming seaweed.

Seaweed farming only started in Tanzania in 1989, but is now an industry of special importance along the coast, both in Zanzibar and in places on the mainland, such as Tanga. The seaweed variety used is called *Eucheuma* and comes from the Philippines. It is used in a range of products, including flavoured milks, jelly, ice cream, preserved meats, toiletries and toothpaste.

Of the seaweed farmers, 90 per cent are women, which gives the industry a special importance. It changes the life of the villages, makes women economically empowered, reduces malnutrition and is reversing the migration from rural villages to the towns.

At villages such as Pajay and Matemwe, several hundred women grow seaweed on strings in the shallow water, almost like vines. It grows very fast in seawater that has a constant temperature of approximately 28°C (82°F), and is ready for harvesting in

Coconuts are an important crop for Tanzanians

Pangani has a Cultural Tourist Programme, and it is possible to use local initiatives to visit *shambas* (small farms) and to try out an *ngalawa* (dugout fishing canoe, the smallest of the *dhows* you commonly see).

Coconuts

The importance of the coconut along the coast is illustrated by the fact that the Swahili language has over 20 words for the different parts of a coconut. Coconuts are found along the coastline both on the mainland and in the islands.

They are not a demanding crop, and coconut palms start to produce after 6 to 8 years, continuing for 50 to 80 years. However, tropical storms ensure that not many trees reach that sort of age.

The trees have numerous uses, including production of *copra* for oil, and also the fibre which comes from the husk. This can be used as fuel for cooking, and the timber itself for various other purposes.

The leaves have traditionally been used for roofing or thatching, which in Swahili is called *makuti*, the traditional roof-covering along the coast. Many tourist buildings, from simple *bandas* to huge public buildings, use *makuti*. The roof construction is very intricate, especially when viewed from inside.

The copra, which is the white flesh of the coconut, is either crushed for coconut oil or sold as oil cakes, and is used in the manufacture of a variety of products, including margarine, vegetable oil, soap and skin-care lotions.

only a few months. It is picked and then dried before sale.

There is competition from the Philippines, Malaysia and Indonesia, and the current price per kilo is very low, but still enough to make a difference. When the fishing is poor, women now even support their husbands.

PANGANI

Pangani is a delightful spot, and those who know it would wish to keep it a secret. It seems destined, at some point, to become a more important tourist destination. The town is very old, and was mentioned in Greek and Phoenician writings 2,000 years ago. It is a peaceful spot with not much to do, but a fine place to 'chill out'.

There is a lovely coral sand beach north of the river mouth, and various remains of its association with slave trading during the Omani period, including the **Slave Prison**, can be found here. Also there is the **German Custom House** that dates from 1916, just before the end of the German period of rule.

The southern coast: Kilwa, Mafia Island and Mnazi Bay-Ruvuma Estuary Marine Park

*If **Kilwa** were in Europe or North America, it would be a major tourist attraction, but as it lies south of Dar in an area devoid of basic infrastructure, almost no one goes there. The problem is its isolation. Southern Tanzania is either an exclusive destination or one for backpackers. However, Mafia Island and Mnazi Bay-Ruvuma Estuary will ensure that once tourist infrastructure is in place, this will be an important area. Mtwara is also a popular weekend retreat for Dar's expatriates.*

KILWA

Kilwa's World Heritage Site status recognises its ruins as the best-preserved ancient Swahili buildings in Africa. There are, in effect, three 'Kilwas': Kilwa Kisiwani (Island Kilwa), Kilwa Masoko (Kilwa Market) and Kilwa Kivinje, the 19th-century slaving port.

History

During the 12th to 15th centuries, Kilwa developed as the greatest trading

Photograph of wall-hanging depicting Kilwa, National Museum

port on the coast of East Africa. Legend tells us that Kilwa was established in AD 975 by Hassan bin Ali, a Shirazi trader. During the next 500 years, it developed as a pivotal point in Indian Ocean trade.

By the time Vasco da Gama arrived at the town in 1498, Kilwa had enjoyed more than three centuries as the pre-eminent trading port on the east coast of Africa. Its buildings were magnificent, and among the largest in Africa south of the Sahara. In 1332, the eminent visitor Ibn Battuta from Morocco said, 'Kilwa is among the most beautiful of cities, and elegantly built.' Already at that time the wealthy lived in stone houses equipped with indoor plumbing.

Prior to the arrival of the Portuguese in 1498, Kilwa had controlled a trade along the coast of East Africa and in the Indian Ocean based on gold, silver, slaves, ivory and myrrh. On his return in 1502, da Gama demanded and received payment of a tribute from the Sultan. Kilwa had effectively become a Portuguese possession, and the Portuguese rapidly began the destruction of Kilwa's trading traditions. By 1513, the centuries-old trading links had been destroyed, and the Portuguese left Kilwa, already in terminal decline. Worse was to come later in the century, when the cannibalistic Zimba people arrived from the vicinity of the Zambezi and in 1587 massacred 40 per cent of the population. After the Portuguese era ended in 1698, Kilwa became a semi-autonomous sultanate, and was involved in slave-trading thanks to a treaty with the French slaver Jean-Vincent Morice.

However, Kilwa's autonomy ended in 1842, the Sultan was exiled and the once-famous city-state was finally abandoned.

Kilwa saw a brief revival of its fortunes at the end of the 19th century, when a mainland port, Kilwa Kivinje, was developed by the ruling Omanis as the terminus for a slave trade from the Lake Nyasa area. Today **Kilwa Kivinje** is a dilapidated town, rather like Bagamoyo, and little more than a fishing village.

Visiting Kilwa

The ruins of Kilwa are on an island (**Kilwa Kisiwani**), about 220km (137 miles) south of Dar. A special

permit is required to visit the ruins, and one can cross over the channel either by leisurely *dhow* or by faster motorboat. You arrive at the fort, which is called the **Gezira** and which was originally built by the Portuguese, reputedly in only three weeks in 1505. The fort was then more or less rebuilt by the Omanis in the 19th century. Apart from some damage caused by the sea, the ruins of the fort are still in good condition.

Nearby is the **Great Mosque**, hailed as one of the greatest Swahili buildings of the medieval period, and certainly one of the finest mosques in East Africa. Its different phases indicate the changes in the fortunes of Kilwa, with the oldest part built in the 12th century, and the prosperity of the 15th-century gold trade resulting in the first major extension.

The small domed mosque is the best-preserved building in Kilwa, and it comes from the late-15th-century period immediately before the arrival of the Portuguese.

Two kilometres (1¼ miles) to the east is the Sultan's Palace, **Husuni Kubwa**, dating from the 14th century, and at one time the largest building in southern Africa. The palace, built mainly in the early 14th century, was three storeys high but was never totally completed, and was lived in for only a few decades. The wealth from the gold trade allowed the palace to be amazingly ornate, and finds of porcelain, pottery and coins show links with the whole of the rest of the known world of that time.

As with Gedi, in Kenya, no one really knows why such a magnificent building was abandoned, especially considering its superb position on a cliff-top. Perhaps it was caused by a crash in the 14th-century version of the stock market. One can only surmise.

Kilwa is well worth a visit, and a little planning and ingenuity will be greatly rewarded. One would have to stay in

Well-equipped diver

Kilwa Masoko, which has a few decent budget guesthouses.

MAFIA ISLAND MARINE PARK

Mafia Island Marine Park, about 130km (81 miles) south of Dar es Salaam, was created in 1995, with support from the World Wildlife Fund, and includes a total area of 822sq km (317sq miles) of the southern end of **Mafia Island**, and the islands of **Chole**, **Jibondo** and **Jiani**. At the time the park was formed, much damage was being caused by dynamite fishing and 'mining' of coral.

Tiger fish

The park includes a wide range of corals, over 400 fish species, hawksbill and green turtles, together with Tanzania's highly endangered dugongs (probably close to being extinct).

On land there are lemurs, wild pigs, various monkeys and dwarf hippos.

The park has also recently been a living example of one of the effects that global warming will bring. During the 1997–8 El Nino event, as a result of sea temperatures becoming unusually warm, large amounts of coral died.

Coral, under threat from global warming

Almost a decade on, though recovery is remarkable, it is still not complete, warning of the mass destruction of coral which will happen if global warming happens as predicted.

Mafia Island is recognised as being one of the world's greatest dive sites, as well as being an important venue for birders and those interested in Swahili historical locations.

Diving at Mafia Island

There are two PADI-accredited centres, Pole Pole Bungalow Resort and Kinasi Lodge. There is a wealth of good diving areas. The favourite dive site is Kinasi Wall, between Kinasi and the sea. Chole Wall, on the northeast side of Chole Island, is also very popular. Kinutia Reef is good for a day trip, with a packed lunch.

Snorkelling is also well catered for, with lots of locations with good corals just below the surface. The visibility is superb (30–40m/98–131ft is normal),

Pemba Beach

and there is a lot to see. Normally used sites include Chole Bay, Blue Lagoon and Kinutia Reef.

Tourist access to Mafia Island is solely by plane, currently with Precision Air. Accommodation is generally in the 'exclusive' range. The best time is usually August to March.

MNAZI BAY-RUVUMA ESTUARY MARINE PARK

The park is east of Mtwara, and occupies the complicated piece of coastline from Msangamkuu Peninsula to the Ruvuma River. It is a collection of various habitats, ranging from mangroves and estuary mudflats, to coral reefs and coral sand shorelines.

It has superb diving and snorkelling, especially on Ruvula Reef, where there is a very steep drop-off. There is one PADI-accredited dive centre, Ten Degree South Lodge.

Msimbati beach is idyllic, with white sands, palm trees and the coral reef. However, the currents here are notorious, and care needs to be taken. As yet there is no development of hotels, but it will no doubt come. There are no fees for the park as there is no park infrastructure set up yet. There is no accommodation in the park, but there is limited accommodation at the Ten Degree South Lodge. Camping is allowed on the beach, and security is said to be good.

TOWNS IN THE EXTREME SOUTH
Mtwara

Mtwara is the most southerly town on the coast of Tanzania and the country's third port. It is in the 'up and coming, watch this space' category. It is one of the locations increasingly favoured by expatriates from Dar es Salaam for short breaks, which is an indication that it has something special to offer. Part of the growth in popularity is certainly due to the coast becoming the Mnazi Bay-Ruvuma Estuary Marine Park, as recently as the year 2000. Though the town is totally unremarkable, the coast is one of the most attractive in the whole country.

However, it is isolated, and the only way to go is to fly. Air Tanzania currently has three return flights a week.

Lindi

Lindi was established in the 18th century as the port for a slave-trade route from Lake Nyasa. The word *lindi* literally means a 'deep channel'.

Flights to Lindi airport, just north of the town, are by Eagle Air from Dar.

There is still a reasonable choice of cheap accommodation, and it is possible to add to the interest of a trip by negotiating a *dhow* to Kilwa or Mafia Island.

There is nothing much to see in Lindi, apart from increasingly dilapidated buildings, but if you can stand a 7- or 8-hour rough 4×4 journey, the **Tendaguru Hills** to the northwest are the site of one of the world's greatest fossil locations. The biggest dinosaur ever found (*Brachiosaurus brancai*) came from here, and is now on display in Berlin. Sadly, commercial fossil hunters continually raid the site.

Fisherman and clear water, Pemba

The southern coast: Kilwa, Mafia Island and Mnazi Bay-Ruvuma Estuary Marine Park

Central and southern towns: Dodoma, Songea, Mbeya and Iringa

Dodoma is the official capital, although in name rather than function. Songea is en route 'to somewhere else' like Mbamba on Lake Malawi. Mbeya is a current success story and its present population is about 400,000, making it the biggest town in southern Tanzania. Iringa is one of Tanzania's most attractive towns and one can do worse than pay a visit en route to Ruaha National Park.

Dodoma

Most folk will visit Dodoma only because they have to pass through it, either on the Central Railway or by road to Lake Tanganyika.

Dodoma is isolated, and hot and uncomfortable from June to October. Its name comes from the Kigogo word *idodomia* ('sinking' or 'sunk').

But, in spite of its isolation, it has relatively good communications in some directions and a good tarmac road to the coast. However, the dirt road to Arusha is sometimes in a poor state.

The town is compact, with everything significant within 1km (²/₃ mile) of the centre. There is a **Central Market**, and an **Anglican** and a **Roman Catholic Cathedral**. The main attraction is the **Geological Survey Museum**.

On Bunge Road, at the Scandinavia Express terminal, one can locate one of Tanzania's most valuable institutions – a first-class bus service.

Geological Survey Museum

Open: 8am–3.30pm. Admission charge.

Songea

Songea is a large and bustling town. The local Memorial Museum commemorates the Maji Maji Rebellion of 1905–6.

Memorial Museum *Open: 8am–7pm.*

Mbeya

The town is located on a high plateau between the Panda Hills and the Mbeya Mountains. It benefits from being on the Tanzam Highway, which links Tanzania and Zambia, and being close to the TAZARA railway. This railway was built by the Chinese in the 1970s, providing an important artery for both Tanzania and Zambia, and opening up the southwest of Tanzania. TAZARA trains run several times a week, but the service is erratic. Check if using the trains. There is a reliable Scandinavia

Express bus service, but you will be on the bus for a very long time from Dar.

If you arrive by train or bus, Mbeya is fairly hassle free. Tourist activities here are largely organised through a cultural tourist programme.

There is plenty of accommodation throughout the price range, but the variety of food is very limited.

There is not much to see in Mbeya itself. Most 'colourful' is the Hanging Tree where the Germans were reputed to have hanged rebels during the 1905–7 Maji Maji uprising.

Climbing Mount Mbeya and **Mount Loleza** is one of the activities organised by Sisi Kwa Sisi (Cultural Tourist Programme). Loleza can be climbed in only about three hours, starting from Hospital Hill. Mbeya Peak can be climbed from the town, but is also worthy of a two-day hike, with an overnight stop at Utengele Country Hotel. This route starts at Mbalizi.

The **Mbozi Meteorite** is a local oddity. Having arrived many hundreds of years ago, it weighed in at about 12 tonnes. It is situated about 70km (43 miles) west of Mbeya on the slopes of Marengi Hill.

Iringa

The town has an elevated position, overlooking the valley of the Little Ruaha River. The folk are friendly, and there are few tourists. As the town is located at an altitude of 1,600m (5,249ft), the temperature is very pleasant, and cool at night. Iringa is the centre of Tanzania's tea-growing business, and has grown up as the market town for those working in tea.

At **Isimilia**, about 15km (9 miles) west of Iringa, next to an amazing free-standing rock pillar, is one of Africa's most important archaeological sites, remnants of the Acheulean age, 60,000 years ago.

Central and southern towns: Dodoma, Songea, Mbeya and Iringa

A magnificent acacia in the Tanzanian bush

Getting away from it all

The mere name of Zanzibar conjures up exciting images of coral sand beaches and of palm trees, of the exotic spice trade and of Arab dhows. It's all there, together with warm temperatures, all year round. Add to this the fascinating architectural heritage of Zanzibar's Swahili culture, and you have a truly remarkable holiday destination.

ZANZIBAR ISLAND

The term Zanzibar may refer to the political entity, to the main island or to the main town. In this introduction we will be thinking of the whole archipelago.

You will almost certainly arrive by air, probably from Dar es Salaam, Arusha or from an airport in Kenya. Most visitors are European, with about three to four times as many Italians as any other national group, followed by British, Scandinavians, Americans and Germans.

Time to visit

Most people tend to come during the dry seasons, but there is no reason why you should not visit Zanzibar at any time of year. The dry seasons are December to February, and June to October. Rain occurs in November (short rains) and April to May (long rains) but is rarely continuous for long, and there is the advantage of fewer visitors and cheaper prices.

Zanzibar's climate is monsoonal, with winds reversing at different seasons, the northeast monsoon from November to March and the southwest monsoon from June to October. Being on the windward side of the island is often preferable, as it gives you the benefit of the moderating sea breezes.

It is never very hot, with temperatures in the range of 26–28°C (79–82°F). However, the humidity can, at times, be uncomfortably high, especially from

A suite at the Bluebay Resort on Zanzibar Island

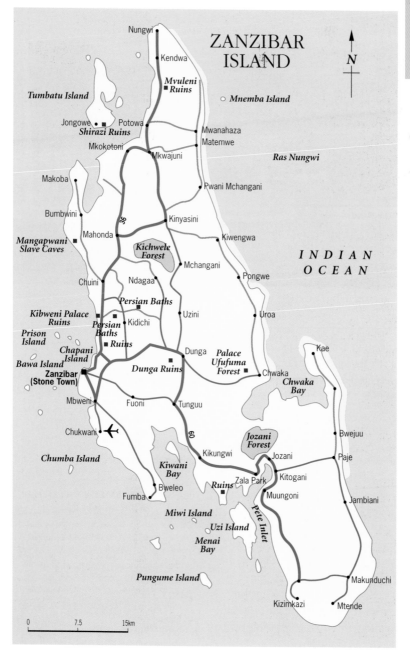

ZANZIBAR ISLAND

N

Nungwi
Kendwa
Mvuleni Ruins
Mnemba Island
Tumbatu Island
Jongowe • Potowa
Shirazi Ruins
Mkokotoni
Mwanahaza
Matemwe
Mkwajuni
Ras Nungwi
Makoba
Pwani Mchangani
Bumbwini
Kinyasini
36
Kiwengwa
Mahonda
Mangapwani Slave Caves
Kichwele Forest
INDIAN OCEAN
Mchangani
Chuini
Ndagaa
Pongwe
Persian Baths
Uzini
Kibweni Palace Ruins
Persian Baths
Kidichi
Uroa
Prison Island
Ruins
Chapani Island
Dunga
Palace Ufufuma Forest
Kae
Bawa Island
Zanzibar (Stone Town)
Dunga Ruins
Chwaka
Chwaka Bay
Mbweni
Fuoni
Tunguu
Chukwani
60
Jozani Forest
Bwejuu
Chumba Island
Kikungwi
Jozani
Paje
Kiwani Bay
Ruins
Zala Park
Kitogani
Fumba
Bweleo
Muungoni
Jambiani
Miwi Island
Uzi Island
Pete Inlet
Menai Bay
Makunduchi
Pungume Island
Kizimkazi
Mtende

0   7.5   15km

The Omani Fort in Stone Town

December to February, and your 'beach cottage in paradise' might come minus either air-conditioning or a fan, making sleeping difficult inside a mosquito net. At these times an onshore breeze is very welcome.

Busy holiday times may also be best avoided, as these are the periods when expatriates from Dar es Salaam, Nairobi and presently Arusha flock to the coast and the islands, making available accommodation scarce.

Also avoid Ramadan, the Muslim month of daytime fasting. Although locals certainly live it up at night, restaurants, bars and even shops may be closed during the day. Ramadan moves 11 days earlier in the calendar annually. It is from 13 September to 12 October in 2008.

Geography

Zanzibar Island lies about 40km (25 miles) off the mainland coast, and is roughly 85 × 30km (53 × 19 miles) in extent. Pemba, to the north, is about 75 × 20km (47 × 12 miles). Also there are dozens of small islands, such as Mnembe and Uzi, many of which are superb diving locations.

ZANZIBAR INTERNATIONAL FILM FESTIVAL

This festival (also known as 'Festival of the Dhow Countries') is held is held in the first half of July and includes music and art as well as film. There are usually about 25 films and the venues are the Forodhani Gardens, the Omani Fort and the Cine Afrique. Other exhibits are in the House of Wonders and the Old Dispensary.

Details are on www.ziff.or.tz

All islands are fairly flat, with the maximum altitude on Zanzibar (Unguja) being only 120m (394ft). The land is generally formed from former coral, some of which is relatively unweathered and is visible on the surface. Coral is the main building stone.

There are fringing coral reefs all round the coast, broken in a few places. The reef is generally a kilometre (1¹/₄ miles) or so off the coast, and there is usually a shallow lagoon between the reef and the mainland. Many areas have gorgeous white sandy beaches. Beyond the reef, the seabed plunges into the depths of the Indian Ocean.

With the coral sand, the lagoon and the reef, normally fringed with coconut palms, for many the Zanzibar coastline is the nearest they will get to their idea of paradise.

Cloves are still the major export of Zanzibar, although seaweed collection has recently become increasingly important.

Tourism is now Zanzibar's biggest industry, even surpassing the spice trade for which it is most famous.

The history of Zanzibar

One would likely visit Zanzibar for one of two reasons, for the beaches and the reefs, or for **Stone Town**, sometimes called the Venice of Africa. As visiting Stone Town is such a historically based experience, in order to understand one's visit more fully, it is good to have some historical knowledge, specifically of Zanzibar.

ZANZIBAR, WHAT'S IN A NAME?

It is good to sort out what the name Zanzibar means at the outset, because it is used in different ways. Zanzibar technically and politically refers to the whole archipelago, the collection of two big islands and many small ones.

But Zanzibar is also used as the name for the main island, which is known as Unguja.

Zanzibar is additionally the name of the main settlement, Zanzibar Town, but the town is also known as Stone Town.

Zanzibar was certainly known to the Greeks and the Romans, and it is believed the Greeks called it by the name Menouthesis. For thousands of years, Arab and Persian sailors navigated the East African coast utilising the monsoon winds, arriving in Zanzibar on the northeasterly and leaving after a few months on the southwest monsoon.

It is believed that Bantu people began to arrive about AD 300–400 from the area of present-day Cameroon. Islamic expansion occurred from the 7th century onwards, and the Sultan of Shiraz established settlements at Lamu, Mombasa, Kilwa and Zanzibar.

The oldest mosque in East Africa was built at Kazimkazi, at the southern end of Unguja in AD 1107, and in the 13th century Zanzibar was minting its own coins. There is evidence of direct trade with China, with India and with ports such as Sofala, further south along the East African coast.

Serena Inn, Zanzibar's former telegraph office

When Vasco da Gama arrived in 1498, he found not savages, but a trading system that had been functioning for at least a thousand years. To 'discover' the route to India, he hired an Omani navigator, Ahmed bin Majid, to show him the way.

Sadly, the Portuguese effect on Zanzibar and its trade was not to embrace it, but to destroy it. The Portuguese received a hostile 'welcome' in Zanzibar, making an alliance with the Sultan of Malindi. Within five years, in 1503, they attacked Zanzibar capturing more than 20 *dhows* and killing 35 people. The Sultan of Zanzibar agreed to pay an annual tribute, and within ten years or so the importance of Zanzibar in the trading scene of the Indian Ocean was gone.

The Portuguese dominated the coast of East Africa for 200 years, and were eventually expelled by the Omanis, who began their raids on the coast about 1650. The Omani Fort, on the waterfront of the Stone Town, was built on the site of the former Portuguese church.

One important development was based on the instruction in the Koran that no Muslim could become a slave, and so began the infamous slave trade, which saw perhaps a million or more Africans captured and sold into slavery. Up to the 18th century, there were perhaps 5,000 African slaves in Oman.

Sultan Said, spices and slavery

By 1800 there were already about 8,000 slaves being brought each year from the mainland and sold in the slave market of Zanzibar. Moreover, the introduction of cloves to both Unguja and to Pemba caused a massive increase in demand for slaves. In 1820 Tabora was established as the inland hub of slave trading for much of the interior.

In 1827 Sultan Said came to Zanzibar and declared that for every coconut tree, there should be three clove trees

THE ZANZIBAR VESPA SYNDROME

Why are there so many scooters on Zanzibar? You cannot help notice that Zanzibar seems overrun by scooters. Apparently this dates back to a recent pre-election period, where the democratic process was 'lubricated' or 'massaged' by cheap loans allowing the populace to buy scooters, motorbikes and, in some cases, cars.

planted, causing a massive increase in the perceived need for slaves.

Though slave trading was abolished in the British Empire in 1833, in Zanzibar it was to continue for another 40 years, and indeed to grow during that period.

In 1840 Sultan Said moved the capital of Oman to Zanzibar, and was henceforth 'Sultan of Zanzibar and Oman', and from about 1850 onwards Zanzibar town became transformed into the Stone Town it is today.

Slavery continued to expand, and in 1841 a slave-trading colony was established at Ujiji on Lake Tanganyika. By the 1850s Zanzibar was receiving up to 15,000 slaves each year, from all over East and Central Africa, anywhere from Angola to southern Ethiopia.

The arrival of the Europeans

The period from the mid-1840s to the end of the 1860s saw the arrival of Europeans in Zanzibar, first the German missionary Johannes Krapf, and later Burton, Speke and eventually Livingstone and Stanley. Mainly they came sponsored by the British Royal Geographical Society, for purposes which now seem almost ludicrous, such as to discover the source of the Nile. But along with their exploratory zeal, the Europeans also continued to pressurise for the abolition of the slave trade.

Getting away from it all

There are scooters everywhere in Zanzibar!

In 1869 the Suez Canal was completed, and in 1872 the influence of Britain was extended by the British India Steam Navigation Company with the establishment of a monthly mail service to Zanzibar. The same year, most of the clove trees in Zanzibar were destroyed in a violent tropical storm, and were never wholly replaced. One year later, in 1873, the British threatened a blockade of Zanzibar if slavery continued, and the Sultan of the time, Barghash, submitted and slave trading came to an end.

Completion of Stone Town

Sultan Barghash began to travel and subsequently brought back to Zanzibar the modern delights of Europe. Stone Town received a supply of clean water, the telephone and electric lighting. The House of Wonders, with all its 'mod cons', was completed, and the roads and general infrastructure were much improved. An undersea telegraphic cable was laid from the present site of Serena Inn to Aden.

In 1880 Zanzibar became a British Protectorate.

Stone Town

Stone Town must be the most visitable historic tourist attraction in Africa south of the Sahara. Completed mainly in the 19th century, but extending back over many centuries, it is a tight-packed collection of multistorey buildings, over an area approximately 800m (2,625ft) at its widest by about 1,500m (4,921ft). It is made mainly of coral 'stone' bound with lime. Within it you will find palaces, houses, about 50 mosques, shops, workplaces and public buildings.

Originally the area formed a separate island, with a tidal creek as its eastern edge. Now the creek, drained and filled in, forms the wide highway. Creek Road is the location of much economic activity.

Sea view of Stone Town with Serena Inn and the House of Wonders

Roman Catholic cathedral, Stone Town

The slave trade

The slave trade is an episode that most would prefer to forget, but it is an important part of Tanzania's history and the scars are still visible today.

The origins of the slave trade

It is believed that slavery began with the various sultanates from the Gulf, which had control over the coastal areas at different times. Certainly African slaves ended up as Persian sailors and pearl divers in the Gulf. Some became soldiers in the armies of Oman and others worked in saltpans in the area that is now Iraq.

Some were domestic slaves; women were sometimes taken as sex slaves. The trade is thought to have been 2,000 years old.

During the second half of the 18th century slavery expanded, largely because of the need for porters to facilitate the increase at that time in the trade in ivory. Later, within the coastal area, slavery also increased as a result of Sultan Seyyid Said setting up clove plantations in Zanzibar and Pemba. In addition, the French used slaves in their newly established sugar and coffee plantations in Mauritius and Réunion.

Mural depicting slave trade, National Museum

Who supplied the slaves?

The most famous slave trader was Tippu Tip (Hamed bin Mohammed) who was the son of an Arab trader, but also the grandson of an African slave. He was born in Zanzibar and traded 1,600km (1,000 miles) inland from the coast, establishing a base on the western shores of Lake Tanganyika. Other traders included the Nyamwezi, who operated around Lake Tanganyika under the leadership of Msiri and Mirambo. They established long-distance trading routes to Mombasa, Kilwa and Zanzibar, but also west to present-day Angola. One of the consequences was to facilitate the spread of the Kiswahili language inland.

The effects of slavery

For the people of the interior, in many parts of Africa, slavery was disastrous. It caused untold misery, social upheaval and economic collapse. One consequence was that villages became much more compact for defence purposes.

Trading also caused the mixing of ethnic groups and the spread of Kiswahili. Some people became enormously wealthy. The wealth from the trade caused a change in society from one based on religious authority to one based on military power.

Tippu Tip, slave trader, National Museum

What is left today?

Bagamoyo was the end of the road for the estimated 10 per cent of slaves who actually survived the trek from Lake Tanganyika to the coast. In Kiswahili, Bagamoyo means 'lay down your hearts', a fitting name for the port through which the majority of an estimated 1.5 million slaves from the interior passed over the years. In 1860 a Catholic mission was established in Bagamoyo, and the missionaries began buying slaves and freeing them, creating the Christian Freedom Village. In 1873 selling slaves was abolished.

In Zanzibar all that remains today is a monument marking the site of Sultan Seyyid Said's Slave Market, founded in 1811, where, in the 1830s and 1840s, 60,000 slaves a year were sold.

Walks: Stone Town

Because Stone Town is such a labyrinth of narrow alleyways, any exploration must be done on foot. Although Zanzibar temperatures never get very high, at times, especially in January and February, the high humidity makes walking for long uncomfortable. So start your walk either early in the day or late in the afternoon. Also, plan several short walks rather than one long one, and enjoy the total ambience of this amazing place rather than assuming each 'attraction' is the only reason for being there.

WALK ONE

1 Forodhani Gardens

The walk starts at Forodhani Gardens, the open space along the central waterfront, and overlooking the busy harbour. Follow the **blue route**. *Forodhani* means 'ship's cargo' or 'place where ships were reloaded'. Here slaves would have been landed before being taken to the market for sale. Until the 1930s, the area was occupied by customs sheds.

After dark the gardens are transformed into Zanzibar's best place to eat out, a great open-air food market. An amazing choice of food is prepared on charcoal stoves – try from scores of possibilities. Maybe start with fresh seafood or *mantabali* – chapatti stuffed with all sorts of fillings.

2 House of Wonders

Look towards Stone Town and you will see Zanzibar's tallest and perhaps most splendid building, the House of Wonders.

At the end of his extravagant building spree, Sultan Barghash's last gesture was to build a palace that was 'out of this world' for its time. It had running water, electricity, telephones and a lift. In its tower is a clock, which you will see displays 'Swahili time' (i.e. 7am becomes 1am, the first hour of daylight). The House of Wonders was joined to two other palaces, Beit al-Sahel, and Beit al-Hukm, by overhead walkways.

A National Museum occupies one room on the first floor and has a variety of exhibits on Stone Town and the rest of Unguja.

Open: Mon–Fri 9am–6pm, Sat & Sun 9am–3pm. Admission charge.

3 Omani Fort

Next door, on the same side of Nyumba Ya Moto Street is the Omani Fort. The fort is a collection of coral-wall defences and towers, with grassy areas in the courtyards. Although only a few metres away from the hustle and bustle of the waterfront, it is a peaceful place to tarry.

The fort was built by the Omanis following their defeat of the Portuguese in 1698, but has rarely functioned seriously for defence. Apart from at times having a small garrison, it has also been a market, a customs house,

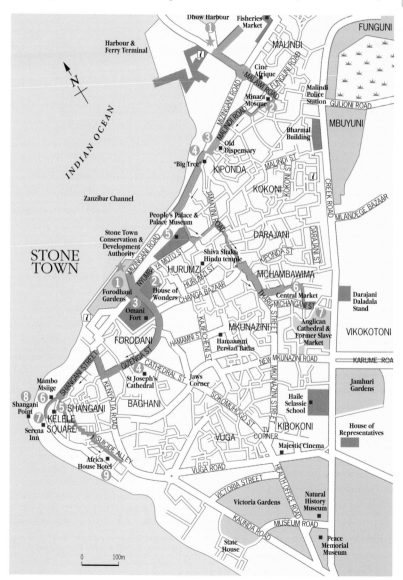

a railway terminus, a jail and a tennis court! Today it serves as **The Zanzibar Cultural Centre**, and there are live concerts on alternative evenings in its charming amphitheatre.

Open: daily 9am–8pm.
Free admission, but there is a charge for evening concerts.

4 St Joseph's Roman Catholic Cathedral

Your walk now requires some navigation, as you wend your way through the alleyways to this cathedral, built between 1896 and 1898. The cathedral lacks the slave market interest of its Anglican counterpart, but that is not to say that the Catholics played any lesser role in the abolition of the slave trade. The Holy Ghost Fathers in Bagamoyo were especially involved, even buying slaves to give them their freedom.

The cathedral is not open to the public except for services, so if you want to go inside, you need to go to Mass!

Freddie Mercury might well be the most important thing about Stone Town for some visitors. He was born Farok Bulsara, and lived here until he was nine, when he went to Britain. Which house was his is open to some debate, and there are several claims. Most likely it is the house now occupied by **Camlur's Restaurant** on Kenyatta Road, but which is presently closed.

5 Kelele Square

Next our walk heads north on Kenyatta Road and into Shangani Street and then south towards Kelele Square. *Kelele* means 'shouting' or 'clamour' in Kiswahili, and refers to the noise from the original function of the square, that of the slave market.

6 Mambo Msiige

As you enter the square, on your right is a house called Mambo Msiige. Originally built by an Arab merchant, in 1850 it was acquired by the Universities Mission to Central Africa as their headquarters, and as such became the home of slavery abolitionist Sir John Kirk. Henry Morton Stanley, the well-known explorer, also stayed here briefly.

7 Serena Inn

Further into the square, on the right, is Serena Inn, one of Zanzibar's finest hotels, and maybe a place for refreshment. The hotel occupies the sensitively restored buildings of the former headquarters of the Cable and

J H SINCLAIR

J H Sinclair arrived in Zanzibar as a young administrator in 1896 and rose to become the British Resident from 1922–4. He was responsible for designing many of the Stone Town buildings at the start of the 20th century. He was known for a peculiar architectural style, a mixture of Islamic and Classical. He designed the Bharmal Building at the end of Creek Road, originally the office of the British Provincial Commissioner and now the office of the Zanzibar Municipal Council. His last building was the Peace Museum, dubbed 'Sinclair's Mosque', which was completed in 1925.

Wireless Company. From here an undersea cable linked Zanzibar and the strategic port of Aden.

8 Shangani Point

Serena is at the extreme tip of Shangani Point and is a good place to photograph the *dhows* as they sweep close to the land as they head south.

As you walk around the point, take a left and you enter Suicide Alley. On your right is the former home of Zanzibar's most infamous slave trader, Tippu Tip. Tippu Tip became enormously wealthy from slaving, and he gathered slaves from as far away as the Congo. The house is still a domestic residence, which is said to be haunted by hundreds of ghosts of former slaves.

9 Africa House Hotel

Finally, continue along Suicide Alley and you cannot miss this hotel, the former exclusive English Officers' Club watering hole, and now renowned as the best place in Zanzibar to see the sunset. It has a rooftop terrace bar, and in the early evening is definitely one of the places to be. Upstairs is a new terrace restaurant.

WALK TWO
1 Dhow Harbour

The walk starts at the harbour and finishes at the Anglican Cathedral and Slave Market. Follow the **orange route**. The Dhow Harbour is something of a revelation. Not only is it still used for sailing dhows, now more often carrying charcoal and mangrove poles from the mainland than spices from India, but it is still the site of the remnant of the outdoor fish market, and is one of the more fly-infested locations on the island. However, early in the morning it is seething with activity, and is memorable in numerous ways. There are some nice photo opportunities, but ask permission before taking close-ups.

2 Minara Mosque

Cross into Stone Town via Malawi Road and you will soon find Minara Mosque, dating from about 1831, one of only four mosques in over 50 which comply with our Western stereotype image of mosques with minarets. Not only that, but the Minara Mosque also has one of only three conical minarets in East Africa, the others being on the Kenyan coast.

The Africa House Hotel

3 The Old Dispensary

Now navigate back to Misingani Road, along the waterfront to The Old Dispensary (also known as Ithna'asheri Dispensary). It is a splendid four-storey building from around 1897, originally constructed by Indian craftsmen for Sir Tharia Topan, who was in charge of customs at the time, and was a banker and a financial adviser. He was also notable in setting up Zanzibar's first non-denominational school.

The building was bought in 1900 and was subsequently used as a charitable dispensary and as a residence for the doctor and his family. It was one of numerous buildings to be renovated by the Aga Khan Trust for Culture and reopened in 1996 as **Stone Town Cultural Centre**.
Free admission.

Shangari Point, Stone Town

4 The Big Tree

Next along the road is the Big Tree, a huge, spreading Indian banyan tree, planted in 1911, and a favourite shady spot for people to meet together.

5 Palace Museum

Beyond the Big Tree you will find the former Sultan's Palace, now the People's Palace, and the Palace Museum. The palace is roughly as it was left when the Sultan fled during the 1964 revolution, minus the odd artefact now to be found in some former politician's front room. It was completed in the 1840s, replacing a former palace on the same site. It became a museum in 1994.

What is generally regarded as the 'number one' exhibit is the room commemorating Princess Salme, who, in 1866, famously eloped with a German merchant, and then was effectively cut off by her family for the rest of her life.
Open: Mon–Fri 9am–6pm, Sat & Sun 8.30am–3pm.
Admission charge.

6 Central Market

Our walk now moves back into the labyrinth of Stone Town to the Central Market (also called Darajani Market), which is located at the junction of Creek Road and Michangani Street. This is an opportunity to immerse oneself in the real, present-day Zanzibar. Here the local people come to buy almost anything, from their charcoal for cooking, to a mobile phone, from fresh shellfish to exotic fruit and vegetables. It is smelly, bustling, colourful and noisy.

The market spills out along Creek Road in both directions.

7 Anglican Cathedral Church of Christ

We end our walk at this church and, next door to the south, at the former **Slave Market**, which was moved here from Kalele Square in 1860.

It is possible to visit some of the underground cells where slaves were kept before being sold. For most visitors it is a sobering experience to witness the cruelty involved in herding frightened slaves into these dark, crowded and miserable conditions.

Slave trading ended in 1873, but domestic slavery in Zanzibar continued until 1917.

The Anglican cathedral was founded in 1873 by the Universities of Central Africa. It contains a number of relics of slavery, including the site of the post where slaves were routinely whipped. Also to be seen in the cathedral precinct is a modern sculpture, showing five figures tied together with a chain brought from Bagamoyo, the mainland end of the slave-trading route.

Slave Market Site. Open: daily 9am–6pm. Admission charge.

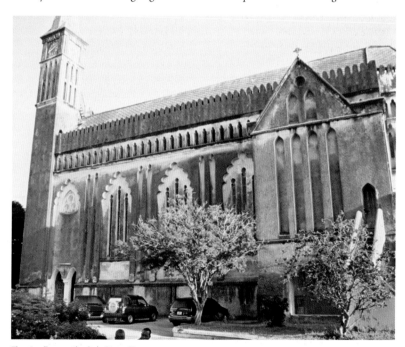

The Anglican cathedral, Stone Town

Day trips from Stone Town

A good day trip involves a visit to the red colobus monkeys of Jozani in the morning, lunch at Kizimkazi and visiting the bottlenose and humpback dolphins off Kizimkazi in the afternoon. Go on an organised trip with a guide. There are also numerous islands not far from Stone Town, which make for some interesting and different days out. Trips can almost always be arranged through your hotel.

JOZANI FOREST AND KIZIMKAZI DOLPHINS
Jozani Forest

Jozani Forest is the largest remaining area of indigenous Zanzibar woodland on the island. In common with other long-isolated island environments in the world, it therefore has many of its own endemic species. The most notable is Kirk's red colobus monkey (*Procolobus kirkii*), of which there are about 2,500 in the Jozani area, roughly a third of the total. Their local name is *kima punji* (poison monkey), coming from the belief that the flesh of the monkeys is poisonous.

There are two groups near to the visitor centre, and you are more or less guaranteed to see them. They behave as though they are totally oblivious to the

There are 2,500 red colobus monkeys in the Jozani area

Family group of colobus monkeys

presence of people, and are very easy to photograph. You end up extremely close to the animals, so only make the visit if you do not have any infection (like a cold) which you might pass on to these rare primates.

Kizimkazi

Kizimkazi is located at the very southern tip of the island, and is Zanzibar's oldest settlement. It was the capital of the island until the 17th century. At Kizimkazi Dimbani it has Africa's oldest mosque and Zanzibar's oldest building. Though the mosque was actually rebuilt on its original foundations in the 18th century, the original north wall with an inscription recording its foundation remains inside.

Non-Muslims are not allowed to enter during prayer times, and women not at all.

The Kizimkazi dolphins are the attraction which draw crowds here. They are to be reliably found every day in the **Menai Bay** conservation area. Whether you want to follow the crowds of boats and tourists and jump in to swim with the humpback and bottlenose dolphins, which frequent the bay, is a matter of personal choice. In more environmentally sensitive areas it

RED COLOBUS MONKEYS

The red colobus monkeys (*Procolobus kirkii*) of Jozani Forest in southern Unguja are a unique subspecies, having been isolated from mainland varieties for over 10,000 years. They show differences in colour and in their calls. At times, the population has been close to extinction, but it presently numbers about 7,500, of which about a third are in the vicinity of Jozani. The threat to the monkeys is the same as everywhere in Africa – the disappearance of habitat as human populations expand.

would seem that such behaviour by tourists would not be acceptable, and you may feel that you want to view the dolphins in a more responsible way. The choice is yours.

TRIP TO MBWENI RUINS FROM STONE TOWN

Mbweni lies just 5km (3 miles) south of Stone Town and makes a popular half- or full-day trip. The ruins at Mbweni are of an Anglican Mission from the 19th century. This was originally the site of a plantation that was run by using slaves. However, the plantation was bought by an Anglican Mission in 1871, and it was initially used as a home for freed slaves. It then became

the site of a girls' school, and remained so until 1920.

A botanical garden was set up by John Kirk, who became British Consul General. He was trained as a botanist and was an avid plant collector. Many of the specimens are labelled, and one can visit the botanical garden alone or with a guide.

What makes the visit so pleasant is that the Protea Hotel, with its excellent food and facilities, is located within the gardens, making for a relaxing day out and a nice venue for lunch.

There is a free hotel shuttle bus five times a day from outside the Omani Fort. First bus leaves at 9.30am.

Dhow-building and repair at Maruhubi

PRISON ISLAND

It is also known as Changuu ('tortoise') Island and lies about 5km (3 miles) northwest of Stone Town.

There are various stories told about Prison Island, especially the idea that it was a sort of Tanganyika 'Colditz', reserved for difficult prisoners. However, it is most likely that its main role was as a quarantine camp, mainly for yellow fever patients.

It has some 19th-century ruins and areas of forest containing Suni antelopes. One of the major attractions is the **Tortoise Sanctuary**. Giant tortoises were brought from the Seychelles in the 19th century and some of the present animals may well be over 100 years old.

One can organise a half- or full-day trip through one's hotel, leaving from Stone Town.

BAWA ISLAND

Bawa Island is 6km (4 miles) west of Stone Town and is the largest of the nearby islands. It has no water and therefore no permanent inhabitants. Also there are no facilities, so take everything with you. It is a nice place for diving, snorkelling or just having a picnic.

The trip can be organised through your hotel and takes from 30–90 minutes depending on the boat.

CHUMBE ISLAND CORAL PARK

Chumbe Island is about 6km (4 miles) south of Stone Town and is usually accessed from Mbweni Ruins.

It was Tanzania's first marine park and contains some of the world's best coral habitat, with over 200 coral species. Almost all the corals found around the Zanzibar coast are represented. There are also over 400 varieties of fish. There is no scuba diving allowed, but it is possible to snorkel.

A boat leaves Protea Hotel, Mbweni Ruins, every day at 10am.

Spice farm, vanilla pods

Tour: the spice tour

*Apart from Stone Town and slavery, there is nothing more 'must do' for the tourist on Zanzibar than something to do with spices, especially cloves. Most visitors combine a **spice tour** with a visit to some of the more famous ruins north of Stone Town such as **Maruhubi** and **Mtoni Palaces** and **Kidichi Persian Baths**.*

One is advised to take an organised tour, although taxi drivers and drivers who come with hired cars all seem to know the ropes very well. Start off for your spice tour after breakfast. Together with lunch and a visit to the ruins, the trip will take until the late afternoon.

In some ways the resulting visit seems more like a designer-tourist event than a visit to where spices are grown commercially. The *shambas* ('small farms') which one can visit are not 'plantations', as one might have

expected, but small, demonstration areas with a whole range of different spices, herbs and fruits all growing together. The visit takes an hour or two, during which you will be taken round the *shamba* and shown the usual range of spices, especially cloves, but also most of the ones you have in your spice rack.

Traditionally the final exhibit is a demonstration of coconut tree climbing, and a refreshment of coconut milk, harvested before your very eyes. Inevitably, as in all good tourist events, you are then given the opportunity of buying a selection of spices as a souvenir.

It is possible you will be left feeling there should be more to it. Where are all the thousands of clove trees?

Maruhubi Palace

Maruhubi Palace ruins are situated only 3km (2 miles) north of Stone Town and you may visit there before your spice tour. This was the palace where Sultan Barghash kept his harem, supposedly

Maruhubi Palace ruins near Mtoni

Mtoni Beach Hotel, north of Stone Town

99 concubines sharing the building with one wife. Sadly, the mainly wooden building was burned down in 1899, and only the foundations and some of the stone pillars remain.

Mtoni Palace

Mtoni Palace, completed in 1832, is close by and was the first official residence of Sultan Seyyid Said. Originally it was extremely ornate and elaborate, occupying two floors and enjoying its own mosque and an extensive garden which was both zoological as well as botanical. It too burned down, this time in 1914, leaving only the mosque standing. The palace had an ignominious end, finishing its days as a warehouse, until it was ultimately destroyed. Little more than the foundations now remains.

Kidichi Persian Baths

Kidichi Persian Baths have survived in much better condition. They too were part of a palace belonging to Sultan Seyyid Said, and built for his second wife, Binte Irich Mirza. They are described as Persian because of the style of their lavish decorations in the carvings, including flowers, birds and date palms. Reproducing images of God's creations would have been forbidden for local Muslims, and the work was almost certainly that of Persian craftsmen.

Ruins open: 8am–4pm. Small entrance charge.

ZANZIBAR TRAINS

You won't find a train on Zanzibar today, but, in the 1880s, Zanzibar had the first train in Africa, when Sultan Barghash had a 0.6m (2ft) gauge line laid from Stone Town to his palace at Chukwani. Between 1905 and 1909 a second line, this time 1m (3ft) gauge, was constructed from the Omani Fort to Bububu, a distance of about 11km (7 miles). Eventually the line was removed and replaced by the motorcar.

Northern Unguja: Zanzibar's coastal areas northwest and northeast

Nungwi was originally a small fishing village, but is now a major resort and likely to grow. Located about 60km (37 miles) north of Stone Town, it is therefore a lengthy transfer from the airport. **Kiwengwa** *is over 60km (37 miles) from Stone Town and, although it is only given a brief mention, it is actually the most important single package holiday location on the island.* **Matemwe** *fishing village lies on the northeast coast of Unguja, around 7km (4 miles) south of Mnemba Island.* **Mangapwani** *is 20km (12 miles) north of Stone Town.*

The northwest peninsula, Nungwi and Kendwa

Tourist facilities at Nungwi are concentrated on either side of the Ras Nungwi peninsula. Although one major tourist guidebook writes off the area as being definitely for backpackers, there is a PADI dive centre at Dive Zanzibar, and a range of good-quality accommodation. Paradise Beach Hotel,

Fishing boats, Matemwe Beach

for example, offers 32 rooms and chalets, all with en-suite facilities and fans. In general, the budget accommodation is on the west of the peninsula and the more upmarket facilities are on the eastern side. There is good diving and snorkelling, as well as sunset *dhow* cruises.

Right at the tip is a lighthouse (not visitable) and a nearby aquarium at Mnarani, where a small tidal lagoon contains green and hawksbill turtles.

Kendwa is 3km (2 miles) southwest of Nungwi and has good beaches and budget hotels.

Kiwengwa

Kiwengwa is the destination for most of the Italian tourists, who make up by far the largest single national group. The holidays offered there are in a number of large complexes and are generally all-inclusive. These developments have been much criticised, both internationally and within Zanzibar. They involve mass, insensitive clearing of land, and visitors there can be totally isolated from the rest of the island.

Generally they occurred because the government wanted short-term financial gain rather than developments which either were environmentally friendly or offered a much better long-term gain for Zanzibar. Two of these resorts burned down in 2001.

They almost all include 5-star facilities. Some, like Blue Bay Beach Resort, have superb sports facilities. Bluebay is also a PADI centre.

The northeast coast: Matemwe

A reef lies about 1km (²/₃ mile) offshore from Matemwe, leaving a shallow lagoon at low tide twice a day. The fringing sand is white and the coconut palms grow back from the beach – 'paradise' in the eyes of many holidaymakers.

Seafood lunch at Mangapwani Beach

During the day, scores of women harvest seaweed in the shallow lagoon, while the men are out fishing in 30–40 small *dhows*. The men 'punt' the *dhows* northwards in the morning, but use their beautiful lateen sails on the homeward journey, providing the tourists with endless photo opportunities.

Matemwe Bungalows lie just south of the village on a low, coral cliff, offering simple but exclusive accommodation and service.

Mangapwani

Part of the journey to Mangapwani ('Arab Shore' in Swahili) is on a very bad road, so allow plenty of time.

It has a nice beach and is worth visiting for two different caves. The first one you see was carved out of the soft coral rock after slave trading with Oman was banned in 1845. It was used again for illegal slaving at the end of the 19th century after the final abolition of all slave trade in 1873.

The second cave is 2km (1¹/₄ miles) further south and is a large, natural cave in the coral. Inside the cave is a large pool. Legend says it was discovered when a slave boy went hunting for a lost goat. All such caves along the coast have a spiritual significance to local people and all contain a variety of offerings to ancestors.

There is no accommodation at Mangapwani, but you can have a nice lunch at **Mangapwani Seafood Grill**.

The coral coast

Coral occurs in warm, clear, shallow tropical water, usually only 30° north and south of the equator. It covers nearly 10,000km (about 6,000 miles) of coastline worldwide in over 100 countries. Coral reefs are the largest structures on the planet that are made by living organisms. Along the east coast of Africa, coral is found all the way from the Red Sea to South Africa. However, along the west coast, because the sea is much colder there, coral is only found in a very narrow strip close to the equator.

Tanzania's coast has fairly continuous coral, broken only where rivers flow into the sea, introducing muddy water, which corals cannot tolerate.

The coral reef

The coral reef has the greatest diversity and is the most productive 'landform' on the planet. One description of coral reefs is that they are 'the rainforests of the sea'. There are over 6,000 species of the coral-forming *Anthosa*, responsible for most coral formation. Coral is created by colonies of creatures called 'polyps' which successively secrete a sort of external skeleton which hardens into the many, intricate calcium carbonate forms we know as coral. A few other life forms also contribute to the reef, especially coralline algae and tubeworms.

Functions of coral

Coral has a number of very important roles within the ecosystem, and the economy:

- It provides food and shelter for a host of fish and invertebrates.
- It protects the coast.

Dhows, coral and Mnemba Island

- Increasingly it is a source of medicines.
- It is an important tourist facility for countries like Tanzania.
- It is an important land-builder in the tropics. Some countries are almost entirely coral.

Threats to the coral

Due to the fact that it is so sensitive to changes in the environment, coral may be a key indicator of the world's ecological health.

Coral is under threat. Some of the threats are natural, such as the damage caused by the storm waves of hurricanes and tropical cyclones. However, many we describe as 'anthropogenic', or manmade.

Coral is very sensitive to changes in the environment, and the increased human activity resulting from population expansion causes numerous direct threats to the coral reef. These include the effects of global warming, especially the rapid rise in sea level, but also the increase in carbon dioxide, to which coral is highly sensitive. Another factor is the occurrence of El Nino, the cyclical major climate 'wobble' which influences temperatures and rainfall globally. It is believed that during the 1998 El Nino, 15 per cent of the world's coral died.

Other factors that contribute to the destruction of coral are an increase in freshwater run-off from the land due to more effective drainage from towns; and high levels of nutrients, insecticides and sewage effluent. Over-fishing, together with extreme and illegal methods such as 'dynamite fishing', resulting in destruction of reefs and a decline in fish, adds to the considerable list of threats to coral's continued survival. Lastly, destruction of the reef by souvenir hunters and by boats landing just may be the last straw.

Tanzania's coral reefs

Tanzania has an abundance of superb reefs in many locations. The most outstanding diving is at Misali Island, though Mafia Island is generally seen as the number-one diving venue in East African waters. Don't miss Mnemba Atoll and numerous fine diving locations around Zanzibar and the other islands.

Eroded coral cliffs at Matemwe

Pemba Island

Pemba is slightly smaller than Unguja and lies to the north. Pemba is mainly made from rock, and has a landscape reaching over 1,000m (3,281ft), with a much more lush vegetation than Unguja. It is visited by very few people, and has relatively few facilities for tourists. However, it is of world importance for one or two activities, and we will mention these.

Almost everyone arrives by air at Karume Airport. Because there are so few visitors, it is best that you make sure of your own onward travel arrangements from the airport. Few tourists use the ferries to Pemba, but it is possible to travel from Dar es Salaam or Zanzibar-Stone Town to the port of **Mkoane**. You can even travel by *dhow* from Tanga, Pangani or Bagamoyo, but such adventurous travel is beyond our present scope.

Cloves

Pemba is synonymous with cloves, the dried flowerbuds of the tree *Eugenia caryophyllata*. They are used in cooking, and clove oil is used in medicines, perfumes and, as many of us know to our pain, in relieving toothache. Until the great storm of 1872, Unguja was the main producer in the world, but when most of the trees were destroyed, and never replanted, Pemba took over, and since then

Freshly picked cloves

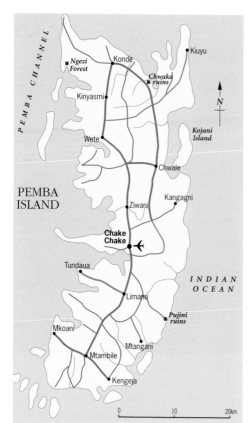

Getting away from it all

almost totally surrounded by coral, often with incredibly steep drops into the depths of the Indian Ocean. Because there are so few tourists, the reefs are largely undisturbed, and the experience is generally idyllic. Water temperatures are invariably about 28°C (82°F) and water visibility ranges from approximately 25m (82ft) to 65m (213ft).

The generally accepted top dive spots are: **Manta Point**, the top of an underwater peak; **Misali Island**, which has very steep cliffs descending to the deep **Emerald Reef**; and **Fundu Reef**. There are five PADI-accredited dive centres (*see Directory on pp164–5*), Dive 7-10, Manta Reef Lodge, Pemba Afloat, Pemba Blue and Swahili Divers. Some details on Dive 7-10, one of the PADI centres, gives a flavour of what most good dive centres will offer.

Dive 7-10 is located at Fundu Lagoon off northwest Pemba. It offers high-class accommodation in 14 bungalow-tents, all in traditional *makuti* style, and with en-suite bathrooms and ceiling fans. Dive boats can take 14 divers each and their 50 knots make for access to a wide range of reefs in a short time.

The centre caters for the whole range of divers, from absolute beginners, to advanced, rescue and divemaster

has produced over 90 per cent of Tanzania's crop.

Clove marketing is controlled by the government, which has kept prices to growers pitifully low, resulting in much poverty on the island, and a demand from the farmers that they have more control over their own livelihood than they presently enjoy.

Diving

Without a doubt, Pemba is one of the top diving locations in the world. It is

Fewer tourists means a more serene diving experience

courses. As well as diving, visitors can also enjoy snorkelling, waterskiing and kayaking. There is satellite TV and excellent international cuisine.

One can expect to see tuna, jacks, wahoo, manta and eagle rays, Napoleon wrasse, as well as sharks and turtles. Due to the currents, most dives are done as drift dives. There is also the possibility of wreck-diving at **Panza Island** at the south end of Pemba.

Witchcraft

Pemba is also infamous for its witchcraft, and is claimed to be a world centre for those into black magic, voodoo and associated activities. How this reputation relates to what's on offer to visitors is difficult to assess

Pemba's ruins

If you begin to get tired of diving and witch-hunting, there are some notable ruins. **Quambalu**, situated on the long and narrow peninsula of **Ras Mkumbuu**, is reputed to be the oldest Islamic town in East Africa. It dates from the 9th century, with most of the ruins being 13th or 14th century. It had a very large mosque, only surpassed by that of Kilwa. Quambalu is another example of a town on the coast of East

Africa that was abandoned for reasons still unknown. Gedi, in Kenya, is another site of deserted ruins.

Punjini is located in the southeast of the island, about 10km (6 miles) from the capital, Chake Chake. It is the remains of the citadel of the 15th- and 16th-century rulers of Pemba, descendants of the original Shirazis, people called the Diba. The ruins are generally unspectacular, though the mosque is best preserved. As the ruins are not signposted, the best way to reach them is to hire a car with a driver, who will certainly know the way.

Misali Island

Misali Island lies about 17km (11 miles) west of Chake Chake, and in 1998 became a protected conservation area. In a report done at the time it was estimated that the fishing grounds around Misali supported 1,600 fishermen from 29 communities. It is therefore important that Misali produces an income to ensure its sustainability as a marine sanctuary. At the moment there are no developments whatsoever on the island, but its rich ecosystem makes it a potential exclusive dive site for the future.

Getting away from it all

There are no developments whatsoever on Misali Island

Shopping

In Tanzania you will come across a huge variety of souvenir crafts for sale. Be sure to check the country of origin though, as some items may have been imported from Far Eastern countries. Nonetheless, you are sure to find a selection of arts and crafts giving you an honest souvenir of your holiday. Almost every hotel and lodge will have its own souvenir shop. Although there are exceptions, very often the range of goods is limited and is the same everywhere. If you want to find more variety, you have to look for it.

What to buy?

Makonde carvings are produced in a variety of genres. They are found especially in Dar es Salaam and Arusha. They vary considerably in scale and price.

Tingatinga paintings follow the colourful style of artist Edward Tingatinga, and are found everywhere, but especially on the coast.

Kikoys and *kangas* are colourful wraps worn by both men and women at the coast. They are probably the most popular souvenirs bought in Dar es Salaam and Zanzibar. They are available everywhere, especially on the beach, in an amazing array of colours and designs.

A range of crafts including tie-dye, batiks, basketwork, soapstone carvings, animal carvings and beadwork are available in many locations.

Maasai beadwork is on sale throughout the country, but be ready to be besieged, whenever you stop anywhere in Maasai territory, by hordes of Maasai women selling their wares.

A range of Tanzanite gems and jewellery is available in a number of reputable shops, chiefly in Dar, Zanzibar and Arusha.

Where to buy?

Dar es Salaam

Mwenge Market is probably the best place to shop in the country. It has scores of small stalls and a super range

Tanzanite gems of all shapes and sizes

of everything. You will find lots of carvings, especially in ebony.

Nyumba ya Sana, meaning House of Art, has lots of paintings, clothes and crafts. It is also a good place to eat at the Bustani Restaurant.

The Slipway is a Western-style shopping mall, but with a mixture of shops selling carvings, paintings and clothes.

Arusha

Cultural Heritage is situated on Serengeti Road. It is a very good craft shop, perhaps number one in Tanzania. With an excellent range and quality, it will ship goods anywhere.

Lookmanji Curio Shop sells wood-carvings, batik and soapstone. The arts and crafts are good quality, but expensive.

Bagamoyo

Bagamoyo Living Art and Handicraft Design Centre is a women's co-operative making a range of fabrics, pots, tie-dye, baskets etc. Buy from the women who make the goods and ensure you support the local people, not a factory in Taiwan.

Zanzibar

This is the place to buy *kikoys*, and you will find them everywhere. Wander round the Stone Town, especially near the Old Fort and be prepared to bargain.

The Gallery Zanzibar

Best souvenir shop in Zanzibar for crafts, spices and books.
Kenyatta Rd.

Memories of Zanzibar

Opposite Shangari Post Office.

Small co-operative of craft shops, Dar es Salaam

Entertainment

Discussing entertainment available for holidaymakers in East Africa is a bit different from other tourist areas, because on many holidays you simply cannot leave your hotel or lodge. On safari, especially in national parks, and in reality almost everywhere else, you cannot go anywhere after dark, and therefore any entertainment must be in house. In addition, if your early game drive starts at 6.30am every day, your body is more likely to be interested in an early night than going out on the town.

On safari

The usual safari entertainment fare centres on Maasai dancing and singing, which most camps arrange on alternate evenings. At many places there is a mini Maasai market after the dancing. On other evenings there may be a mixture of wildlife and cultural talks. The majority of lodges and camps also have a camp choir, mostly in demand for birthdays, which they help guests celebrate very well.

In Zanzibar and at the coast

It is possible to go out in the evening, though once again the vast majority of guests do not leave their hotel after dark. In some places, especially Stone Town in Zanzibar and in much of downtown Dar es Salaam, one is generally advised not to go walkabout once the sun is down.

Traditional music

Traditional music can be heard at different times in Stone Town, Zanzibar. Most famous is *Taarab*, a mixture of music from Africa, the Middle East and India. Stone Town has two main groups, Nedi Ikwan Safaa and Mil na Utamaduni, that perform at different events.

Cocktails at Zanzibar Beach Resort

Golfing lodge near Arusha National Park

The Omani Fort is the most regular cultural centre, with a performance in the Amphitheatre on alternate evenings, with access from Forodhani Gardens, so that you can eat alfresco before or after the performance.

TAARAB MUSIC

Taarab is the name given to music that was originally played at the court of Sultan Barghash. One story is that he sent a musician to Egypt, to learn to play the *qanum*, a sort of zither. What the musician returned with was a combination of sounds from India and Indonesia, as well as the Arab countries.

Today *Taarab* musicians play a range of instruments such as violin, cello, accordion and percussion, as well as regional instruments such as *ney* and *oud*.

The first recorded *Taarab* musician was Siti bin Saad, in the 1940s.

There is traditional music every week at Village Museum (*Wed–Sun afternoons*) and Nyumba ya Sanaa (*Fri evenings*).

Modern music

Dar es Salaam is undoubtedly Tanzania's number one modern-music scene with music at a wide variety of clubs and bars every evening. Check up in *Dar es Salaam Guide* or in the *Swahili Coast Guide*, both free.

The best time for non-stop modern music is immediately after Ramadan, during the festival Idd al Fitr. Ramadan dates change every year, so do check.

If you do go out to Dar's equivalent of clubs and pubs, generally take a taxi, don't walk, and leave your valuables behind.

Children

Tanzania is not yet the place where there are loads of things for children to do. So it is best to ensure that the sort of holiday you plan with children specifically includes the sorts of things they will enjoy and which will keep them happy.

In general, small children and babies are not encouraged on most safari holidays. Apart from the possibility of long, dusty (and boring-for-children) journeys, keeping quiet watching animals is just not the sort of environment where children can behave suitably.

Go sailing at Fundu Lagoon on Solkattan

Similarly, Tanzania is the sort of place where it is likely that you may have a 'tummy problem' for part of your holiday, and where there is a significant exposure to malaria.

Things for children to do
Watersports and the beach
Almost all good hotels will have pools, and many of them are located on the beach. Possibly with children you might consider this essential.

Expect that children's holidays on the coast will be centred on the water. Snorkelling is possible almost everywhere, and older children can try scuba diving. In addition, in some places a variety of other activities are possible such as sailing and windsurfing.

Blue Bay Beach Resort in Kiwengwa, Zanzibar, offers a modern fitness centre, floodlit tennis court, scuba-diving centre, windsurfing, canoes and sailing boats, table tennis, snooker and billiards, and *boules*.

Dolphin watching

Dolphin watching is a reliable holiday activity all year round near Kizimkazi, in the southwest of Unguja Island. There are about 150, mainly bottle-nosed, with some humpbacked dolphins, and the area is an important dolphin calving-ground. On occasion it is also possible to swim among the dolphins if this is something you wish to do.

Exploring rock pools

Twice a day, at low tide, many children find the age-old activity of exploring the rock pools on the beach absolutely fascinating. Just remember that it is against the law in Tanzania to remove any 'souvenirs'.

Horse riding

Older children who are competent riders may find a safari on horseback just the holiday they might enjoy. *Check for possibilities in the sports section on p166 of the Directory.*

Viewing red colobus monkeys

Children will also enjoy the extremely reliable red colobus viewing at Jozani Forest, south of Stone Town.

Warning

With all outdoor activities, especially with children, be aware of the extreme dangers of sunburn in low latitude areas. Keep exposure to the sun brief, cover up as much as possible and use high-factor sun block.

Fishing is an alternative entertainment for children

Sport and leisure

Certain sports attract the attention and interest of visitors, and others are much less relevant than in developed countries. At the coast, watersports are important, and inland there is a mixture of the highly active pursuits, such as mountaineering, and the relatively passive pursuits, such as birdwatching.

Diving and watersports

The coast of Tanzania is made for diving. There are well-known coral reefs in many locations such as Zanzibar, Pemba and Mafia Island, together with hundreds of lesser-known places, such as the small islands north of Dar es Salaam, or many places near the Mozambique border.

The best diving time is November to March, when the water is clearest and the sea is calm.

There is a range of diving offered, from absolute beginner to Divemaster, the top qualification. Make sure you choose a diving company that is a member of PADI (Professional Association of Diving Instructors). You may dive purely for pleasure, or you can give some structure to your holiday by doing a course. There are six levels, starting with 'Discover Scuba'.

The following is a selection of companies offering diving using highly qualified instructors.

Dive boat off Matemwe

Horse riding at Mufindi Highlands

Dive 7-10

Gold Palm PADI dive centre. 'The epitome of the barefoot paradise' on west coast of Pemba.
www.fundulagoon.com

Jan de Villiers

PADI accredited. Offering full range of courses to Divemaster.
Mafia Island. Only radio phone.
chole@intotanzania.com
www.cholemjini.com

One Ocean

PADI accredited. Offering full range of courses to Divemaster.
Kenyatta Rd, Zanzibar.
Tel: (024) 223 8374, fax: (024) 225 0496.
oneocean@zanlink.com
www.zanzibaroneocean.com

Pole Pole

Mafia Island Marine Park PADI courses from beginner to Divemaster.
www.polepole.com

Swahili Divers

PADI accredited. Offering full range of courses to Divemaster.
The Mission Lodge, Chake Chake, Pemba.
Tel: (024) 245 2786.
swahilidivers@intafrica.com
www.swahilidivers.com

Birdwatching

Tanzania offers birdwatchers enormous possibilities, with over 1,100 recorded bird species. The best time is during the Northern Hemisphere winter between November and March, when both the migrants and the endemic species are available.

There are many suitable sites, ranging from mountain areas like the Usambaras to the savannah-lands of the national parks such as Tarangire. Recently, roseate terns, one of the rarest seabirds, returned to breed at Chumbe Island after 12 years' absence.

Horse riding

Horse riding is possible as a mounted safari. Companies offering equestrian safaris include the following:

Equestrian Safaris
Exploring on horseback in remote places.
Arusha. Tel: (0744) 595 517.
posthest@yahoo.com
www.safaririding.com

Farasi Safaris
Riding safaris near Manyara.
India St, Arusha.
Tel: (0411) 364 388.
info@farasisafaris.com
www.farasisafaris.com

Fishing

Sea fishing is available at most places, such as Zanzibar, Bagamoyo, Mafia Island and Pangani. There is a wide range of fishing available, each variety with its own best season.

Freshwater fishing is possible in all the lakes and in some rivers such as the Rufiji.

Zanzibar Dive Centre

Fishing tuition, Rubondo Island

Keeping fit

If you need to work out on holiday, you do not need to miss out. There are gyms in several towns, but your best selection is in Dar es Salaam. They include:

The Fitness Centre
Chole Rd.
Tel: (022) 260 0786.

Ocean Fitness
The Gymkhana Club.
Tel: (022) 212 2331.

Golf

There are no really good golf courses in Tanzania.

Mountaineering and trekking

An example of an ascent up Kilimanjaro is covered in depth in the *Destination Guide, pp79–82*. In Tanzania there is not only Africa's biggest mountain, but many other peaks and ranges for mountaineering, trekking and rock climbing.

Warning: Though Kilimanjaro is probably the easiest big mountain in the world to climb, you must **take it**

Ballooning in the Serengeti

very seriously. The problems associated with **altitude sickness can be fatal**. Always plan your trip through a reputable company.

Some of the companies that can arrange your expedition are listed below. All these are in Moshi, at the northern base of Kilimanjaro.

Ahsante Tours and Safaris
Tel: (027) 275 0479.
www.ahsante.com
Ameg Lodge
Tel: (0744) 058 268.
www.ameglodge.com
Keys Hotel
Tel: (027) 275 2259.
www.keys-hotel.com
Mauly Tours and Safaris
Tel: (027) 275 0730.
www.glcom.com/mauly

MEM Tours and Safaris
Tel: (027) 275 0669.
www.memtours.com
Samjoe Tours and Safaris
Tel: (027) 275 1484.
samjoe@yahoo.com
Zara International
Tel: (027) 275 0011.
www.kilimanjaro.co.tz

Young boys playing a traditional game near Africa House, Stone Town, Zanzibar

Food and drink

As a general rule, holidaymakers, either on safari or at the beach, will eat in their lodge or hotel, where the standard of food is usually very good. However, in Dar es Salaam and Zanzibar there are other options. Most hotels offer a range of international cuisine, and almost all cater well for vegetarians.

If you prefer to eat out, Dar offers the widest range, with about ten Chinese restaurants, even more Indian, about six Italians, four Japanese, and even a choice of Portuguese, Korean and Danish.

Away from Dar, Zanzibar and Arusha, other than in lodges and tourist hotels, vegetarian options will be limited and simple, though not impossible.

In Dar there is a growing takeaway range, with Debonairs' Pizzas leading the way.

Luxury living in the wilderness

Star rating

The price indication is for a three-course meal for one, excluding drinks.

★ Under $10
★★ $11–$18
★★★ $19–$35
★★★★ Over $35

This is purely a guide.

DAR ES SALAAM

Addis in Dar ★★−★★★
Excellent Ethiopian food.
Ursino St.
Tel: (0741) 266 299.

Baraza Bar and Grill ★★
Mixed European-Indian-Chinese. Good seafood.
Holiday Inn.
Tel: (022) 266 7927/7188.

Debonairs' Pizza (Takeaway) ★
Tel: (0784) 783 377 or (022) 212 2855/6.

Jan's Trattoria ★★
Italian. Good pizzas, pastas and grills.
Kimweri Ave. Tel: (0744) 295 709 or (0744) 282 969.

Mövenpick Royal Palm Hotel

Has a whole range of good eating places:

- **Serengeti Restaurant** ★★★—★★★★

  Probably the best restaurant in town.
- **Tradewinds** ★★★

  An excellent steakhouse.
- **99ers** ★★★

  First-class salad bar.
  Ohio St. Tel: (022) 211 2416.

Sawasdee Restaurant ★★★

The restaurant with the best view (9th floor).
New Africa Hotel. Tel: (022) 117 051.

The Slipway ★—★★★

Food court with usual wide range of specialities side by side. Includes 'The Pub' which serves food all day, from breakfast to dinner.
Msasani Peninsula.

ARUSHA

Egina Africa Pizza ★

Small café. Popular for breakfasts.
Levolosi St, Kaloleni. Tel: (027) 250 7203.

Mambo Café ★★

Italian food. Nice ice cream.
Old Moshi Rd.

Mezza Luca ★★

Good Italian food.
Moshi Rd. Tel: (027) 254 4381.

Moshi

China Garden ★

Chinese and Thai food; garden atmosphere.
Taifa Rd. Tel: (027) 55873.

El Rancho ★

Indian, with a good vegetarian menu.
Off Lema Rd. Tel: (027) 55115.

Golden Shower ★

Range of food, served in a garden.
Dar es Salaam Rd.

ZANZIBAR

The hotels all have good restaurants, and visitors will do well to 'eat in'. However, there are some other good eating places.

Africa House ★

Best burgers and chips.

Shangani Rd. Tel: (024) 223 0708.

Emerson and Green ★★★—★★★★

Traditional atmosphere, with excellent food and music. Book well in advance.
236 Hurumzi St. Tel: (0747) 422 3266.

Kidude ★★

Claims the 'best lunch' in town.
236 Hurunzi St.

Mercury's ★★★

Dine right on the waterfront, opposite the Old Fort.
Tel: (024) 223 3076.

Monsoon Restaurant ★★★

Swahili restaurant. Live music Wed and Sat.
Shangani Rd. Tel: (0747) 411 362.

The Dhow ★★★

Eat on board a traditional *dhow* moored in the harbour.

Selection of fish for sale at the Fish Market

Hotels and accommodation

There are adequate hotels in the main centres such as Dar es Salaam and Zanzibar, and a smaller range in towns like Arusha and Moshi, but elsewhere there are luxury lodges and hotels scattered around. There are places in most towns at the bottom end of the market, but nothing in the middle range. At the top end of the market, expect to pay in US dollars or pounds sterling.

Dar es Salaam

African Sky
Millennium Hotel
Handy for airport.
Conference facilities.
Tel: (022) 277 4588.
www.africanskyhotels.com

Belinda Ocean Hotel
Budget hotel.
Jagwani Beach. Tel: (022) 264 7552. belinda@ africaonline.co.tz, www. belindaoceanresort.com

Golden Tulip
Luxurious new hotel next to the Indian Ocean; 90 rooms.
Toure Drive, Msasani Peninsula. Tel: (022) 260 1442, goldentulip@ afsat.com, www. goldentuliptanzania.com

Holiday Inn
New, located near city centre. Big range of facilities, superb views.
Garden Ave. Tel: (022) 213 7575, fax: (022) 213 9070. www.holidayinndar.com

Harbour View Suites
Self-catering. Fitted out to international standards. All rooms with internet. Convenient business location.
Tel: (022) 212 4040. www.harbourview-suites.com

Hotel Sea Cliff
86 rooms. Superb location; great facilities, especially for sport.
Toure Dr, Msasani Peninsula. Tel: (022) 260 0380, fax: (022) 260 0476. www.hotelseacliff.com

Kilimanjaro Hotel Kempinski
Downtown Dar, overlooking Indian Ocean and port. Excellent service.
Tel: (022) 213 1111. www.kempinski-daressalaam.com

Lazy Lagoon Private Island
Idyllic beach resort, north of Dar. Ideal honeymoon location.
Tel: (255) 784 237422. www.tanzaniasafaris.info

Mövenpick Royal Palm Hotel
Stylish and expensive, central location. Very good food in several restaurants. 200 rooms.
Tel: (022) 211 2416. info@royalpalmdar.com www.movenpick-hotels.com

New Africa Hotel
Central Dar, overlooking harbour. Wide range of restaurants and bars.
Tel: (022) 211 7050. www.newafricahotel.com

Q Bar and Guest House
Budget hotel. Only 6 rooms, basic and cheap, but clean and good value. *Msasani Peninsula. Tel: (022) 260 2150. qbar@hotmail.com*

White Sands Hotel
Indian Ocean location. Hotel and conference centre. Refurbished. *Tel: (022) 264 7620. www.hotelwhitesands.com*

Arusha
Moivaro Coffee Plantation
Colonial-style thatched cottages; internet access. *Tel: (027) 255 3242. reservations@moivaro.com*

Serena Mountain Village Lodge
Lovely garden location, views of Mt Meru and Kilimanjaro; set in 40 acres of coffee plantation. *Tel: (027) 255 3313, fax: (027) 255 3316. mtvillage@serena.co.tz, www.serena.co.tz*

Tanga and Pangani
Pangani River Hotel
40 rooms in 9 cottages. Super location, with good food; plenty of outdoor activities. *Tel: (027) 264 5280/2124.*

proteapangani@ africaonline.co.tz, www.proteahotels.com

Zanzibar
Hotel Kiponda
Budget hotel, located in former harem; some en-suite rooms. *Tel: (024) 223 3052. hotelkiponda@email.com*

236 Hurumzi
Elegant grandeur in restored palace, in the heart of Stone Town. *Tel: (0777) 423 266. www.236hurumzi.com*

La Gemma Dell' Est
This resort works hard to blend in with Indian Ocean environment. *Tel: (024) 224 0087. www.planhotel.com*

Ras Nungwi Beach Hotel
Northern Zanzibar. Small luxury hotel. 5-star food. *Tel: (024) 223 3767, fax: (024) 223 3098. www.rasnungwi.com*

Serena Inn
Flagship hotel; highest class, with excellent food. *Shangani. Tel: (024) 233 1015, fax: (0741) 333 170. Central reservations, Serena: Tel: (027) 250 4155/4058. reservations@serena.co.tz, www.serena.co.tz*

Tembo Inn
Restored Omani mansion; sophisticated; no alcohol. *Shangani. Tel: (024) 223 3005. tembo@zitec.org, www.tembohotel.com*

The Africa House Hotel
Former royal residence, now beautifully restored. Best sunsets in Zanzibar. *Tel: (0774) 432 340. www.theafricahouse-zanzibar.com*

Katavi National Park
Katavi Wildlife Camp
Extreme luxury four-tents-only camp, hosted by professional zoologist. *Tel: (0744) 237 422. fox@tanzaniasafaris.info, www.tanzaniasafaris.info*

Lake Manyara National Park
Lake Manyara Serena Lodge
67 rooms, all with views across the park. *Tel: (027) 250 4155/4058, fax: (027) 250 8282. reservations@serena.co.tz, www.serena.co.tz*

Lake Manyara Tree Lodge
Only lodge actually in the park. *Tel: South Africa +27 (11) 809 4300. www.ccafrica.com*

Mikumi National Park

Foxes Safari Camp

Small bush camp with only eight tents; personalised service.
Tel: (0744) 237 422.
fox@tanzaniasafaris.info,
www.tanzaniasafaris.info

Ngorongoro Conservation Area

Ngorongoro Crater Lodge

One of the outstanding safari lodges; unashamedly luxurious.
Tel: South Africa +27 (11) 809 4300.
www.ccafrica.com

Ngorongoro Serena Lodge

Serious conservation architecture, with a building skilfully blended into the landscape; superb views over the crater.
Tel: (027) 250 4155/4058.
reservations@serena.co.tz,
www.serena.co.tz

Ngorongoro Sopa Lodge

The only lodge on the eastern crater rim, so the best for sunsets; has its own crater-floor access road.
Tel: (027) 250 0630.
info@sopalodges.com,
www.sopalodges.com

Octagon Safari Lodge

Located near to main gate to Ngorongoro in nice garden environment.
Tel: (027) 254 8311.
www.octagonlodge.com

Ruaha National Park

Mwagusi Safari Camp

Exclusive tented camp on the Mwagusi River.
Tel/fax: UK +44 (20) 8846 9363.
tropicafrica.uk@virgin.net

Ruaha River Lodge

22 stone and thatch *bandas* on banks of the Great Ruaha River in the National Park.
Tel: (0744) 237 422.
fox@tanzaniasafaris.info,
www.tanzaniasafaris.info

Selous Game Reserve

Belo Belo Camp

Exclusive and remote stone cottages.
Tel: (022) 260 0352/3/4,
fax: (022) 260 0347.
oysterbay-
hotel@twiga.com

Selous Safari Camp

Classic bush camp; waterfront location; boat trips; excellent food.
Tel: (022) 213 4802,
fax: (022) 211 2794.
info@selous.com,
www.selous.com

Serengeti National Park

Grumeti River

A CC Africa luxury camp, located on the northern side of the Grumeti River. Low key, luxurious.
Tel: +27 (11) 809 4300.
www.ccafrica.com

Kirawira

Luxury tents, located in the Western Corridor. Serena owned with usual high standards; exclusive.
Tel: (027) 250 4155/4058,
fax: (027) 250 8282.
reservations@serena.co.tz

Klein's Camp

Another CC Africa luxury camp. Located just outside Serengeti National Park, northeast of Lobo. Great food, lots of attention to detail.
Tel: +27 (11) 809 4300.
www.ccafrica.com

Kusini Camp

Isolated in southwest Serengeti, a traditional African safari experience.
www.
abercrombieandkent.com

Mbalageti

New luxury camp overlooking Mbalageti valley in west-central Serengeti.
www.mbalageti.com

Mbuzi Mawe
New Serena luxury camp, between Seronera and Lobo.
reservations@serena.co.tz

Ndutu Safari Lodge
Located in Ngorongoro Conservation Area, but functionally a Serengeti camp. 32 rooms; friendly atmosphere.
Tel: (027) 250 6792/8930, fax: (027) 250 8310.
ndutugibbs@habari.co.tz

Sasawa Hill Lodge; Sabera Plains Tented Camp; Faru Faru River Lodge
New ultra-luxurious lodge and camp accommodation from South Africa. Located in Grumeti Reserve.
www.grumetireserves.com

Serengeti Sopa Lodge
Large lodge with 100 rooms; good game-viewing area.
Tel: (027) 250 0630, fax: (027) 250 8245.
info@sopalodges.com
www.sopalodges.com

Tarangire National Park

Boundary Hills
Small, lovely hilltop location on edge of national park.

Tel: (0744) 470 447.
eastafricasafaris@habari.co.tz
www.eastafricasafari.info

Naitolia
Tiny, isolated; best for experienced travellers.
Tel: (0744) 470 447.
naitolia@tarangireconservation.com
www.eastafricasafari.com

Hotel and lodge chains' websites

CC Africa
www.ccafrica.com

East African Safaris
www.eastafricansafari.com

Fox Tanzania Safaris
www.tanzaniasafaris.info

Gibbs Farm Safaris
www.gibbsfarm.net

Halcyon Africa
www.halcyonafrica.com

Hoopoe Safaris
www.hoopoe.com

Protea Hotels
www.proteahotels.com

Selous Safari Company
www.selous.com

Serena Lodges and Hotels
www.serena.co.tz

Sopa Lodges
www.sopalodges.com

Camping

There are generally three options in Tanzania:

• permanent campsites which are organised by your tour operator
• so-called special campsites, which are temporary, usually in reserves and national parks, and usually exclusively occupied by your safari company
• public campsites, usually provided with toilets and cooking facilities.

Camping at Ngorongoro
There are two public campsites on the southwestern crater rim, plus numerous special campsites. All are bookable at the NCAA offices either at Ngorongoro or in Arusha.

Camping in Serengeti
Serengeti has public campsites at the Ndabaka gate in the west, at Seronera, and at Lobo. All are unfenced against wildlife.
    Serengeti has many special campsites. There is also hostel-type accommodation at the TANAPA rest house, Seronera. Booking is through TANAPA in Arusha or at Seronera.

The TAZARA railway

The authorities in Tanzania and Zambia tried to persuade the world that TAZARA (Tanzania and Zambia Railway Company) sounded better, but the ease with which TANZAM rolls off the tongue has made it permanent. This is the name of the 1,860km (1,156-mile) railway from Dar es Salaam to Ndola in Zambia.

Cecil Rhodes, the British-born colonialist and founder of Rhodesia, now Zimbabwe, dreamed of a railway from Cape Town to Cairo. Though the dream still has great gaps in it, on 14 July 1976, a further 1,860km (1,156 miles) of railway was added to the journey which is so far possible.

The building of the railway, by far the greatest in post-colonial Africa, was inspired by the unilateral declaration of independence made by Ian Smith's Rhodesia (now Zimbabwe) in the mid-1960s. During that time Zambia was cut off from its traditional links to the sea, and even in normal times, one of its major routes was through South Africa, still under apartheid. For years, truck drivers had to struggle with potholed roads and broken axles. Insufficient and inadequate road tankers were supplemented with huge butyl petroleum containers. To construct the railway that was needed was far beyond the means of Tanzania, consistently one of the 25 poorest countries in the world. So, in the middle of the Cold War, much to the shock of countries like Britain and the USA, the Communist Republic of

Decaying rolling stock at the railway station, Dar es Salaam

Tazara headquarters

China came forward with design, financing and building of this railway in the heart of Africa.

The work was started in 1971 and was completed in 1976. In Zambia the track is 110cm (3ft 6in), the same as in Zimbabwe and South Africa. In Tanzania it has a 1m (3ft 3in) gauge, conforming with the Tanzanian system and the rest of East Africa.

Who uses the railway?

The railway was built to facilitate Zambian trade through Dar es Salaam, and although apartheid has gone from South Africa, and Zimbabwe is an independent country, this trade is still important for the railway. In June 2003, the Konkola Copper Mining Company confirmed its continuing intention to make the TANZAM line its preferred export route.

Cape Town to Dar es Salaam

Rohan Voss had dreamed of a train journey which he believed could become the most famous in the world, Cape Town to Dar es Salaam, and in June 1993 his dream came true. This was 17 years after the completion of the TANZAM line. He named his train 'The Pride of Africa'. The journey takes 13 days to complete the 6,100km (3,790-mile) journey, and passengers alternately enjoy breathtaking train travel with stopovers in 5-star locations such as the Victoria Falls Hotel.

In Tanzania the route passes through territory almost inaccessible by means other than the railway. It enters the country at Nakonde/Tunduma, midway between the lakes Tanganyika and Nyasa, passes the domed volcanic cone of Mount Mbeya, and then negotiates the tunnels and switchbacks of the Udzungwa Mountains.

On the last day 'The Pride of Africa' passes through the enormous wilderness of Selous, the biggest game reserve in Africa, and then on to Dar es Salaam.

Memorial to Tazara railway workers, Dar

Practical guide

Arriving

All arriving passengers must have a valid passport and a return ticket.

Presently most nationalities require visas that may be obtained by applying in person or by post to any Tanzanian Embassy, High Commission or Consulate. Apart from a few specified nationalities (check) you may also obtain your visa on arrival. If you do this, ensure you have either US dollars or UK pounds, as you may not use any other currencies.

Immigration may be time-consuming, but normally you will encounter no problems bringing in items for personal use such as laptops, binoculars, cameras etc.

By air

There are a number of scheduled carriers from Europe and the Gulf area, but no 'budget' airlines. Arrival is either by the new Kilimanjaro International Airport or through Dar es Salaam, which is more suitable for coastal or Zanzibar holidays, but less so for safaris. Carriers include KLM, British Airways, Gulf Air, Emirates, Ethiopian Airlines, Egypt Air and Swiss Airlines.

Many travellers find it more convenient to use Nairobi as their hub airport, and to travel to northern Tanzania by road, or using the local carriers such as Regional Air or Precision Air.

Camping

Do-it-yourself camping is a viable option in Tanzania, except on any of the islands, where there is no camping allowed. However, in general, facilities provided are minimal or non-existent and are also not much related to what you pay. Book through TANAPA HQ.

At some sites firewood is provided, but not always. You may be prohibited from foraging for firewood in some locations and will be specifically required to use a gas stove. Check when you book.

Camping in national parks among the animals may seem daunting to first-timers, but is generally very safe. Although there are plenty of stories of lions wandering through the campsite, there are very few instances where campers have been in danger. As with most things, common sense is a valuable commodity.

Safari camp tent

Children

There are two different scenarios concerning children on holiday in Tanzania.

• On the coast, and in Zanzibar and Pemba, it is totally realistic to have children on holiday. The beaches are superb, and almost all hotels have pools. There are lots of things to do.

• On a safari holiday, taking young children is not advised and babies are positively excluded. The problem for most children is that safari holidays, except by plane, involve long, hot drives. Even on game drives the initial excitement wears thin with some children and they get bored, which may be difficult for you, but even worse for fellow travellers in the same vehicle. Babies are not allowed on safari holidays for a number of reasons.

See also Directory, p162.

Climate

Tanzania lies only a few degrees south of the equator, and the climate is therefore tropical. In reality, because of differences in altitude, the weather varies considerably between coastal locations like Zanzibar and inland or highland locations such as Ngorongoro.

The coast is hot all year, with daytime maximum temperatures of about 30–35°C (86–95°F). In the period January to March, added to the temperature is high humidity, so this is the least popular time with some people. Inland, most temperatures during the day are slightly cooler at about 25°C (77°F).

In the evening and at night, coastal temperatures may drop only a few degrees (it never gets cold), but inland it may be positively cool. In the mountains, the altitude also modifies the climate, so that snow begins to appear at about 5,000m (16,404ft).

There are two rainy seasons, which tend to merge into one in southern Tanzania. The long rains generally fall from March to May, and the short rains in November and December.

In the extreme south, the rainy season is approximately from December to April.

For the rainfall and temperature charts, see p8.

Crime

Hardly any tourists in Tanzania have been involved in incidents of serious crime. However, in a country with so much poverty, and in towns and cities swelled with unemployed migrants from the countryside, some petty theft is inevitable. The problem areas are in 'downtown' parts of towns and cities at all times, but especially at night.

The beach is also a target, especially when holidaymakers are paying scant attention to their possessions.

The advice is to behave sensibly:

• Do not flaunt your wealth.

• In crowded areas, remove watches and jewellery.

• Keep valuables in the hotel safe.

- Avoid carrying too much cash.
- Keep your credit cards and your pin number separate at all times.
- Keep a note of serial numbers etc., and keep cards and traveller's cheques separate, in case you do have a problem.
- When swimming, do not leave all your things unattended on the beach or by the pool.
- Avoid walking in downtown areas at night.
- Lock your hotel room.
- Do not leave items that might attract thieves next to open windows.
- If you do experience theft or crime, report it to the police (you will need to do this for insurance claims).

Customs regulations

Drugs

There are stiff penalties for drug dealing. If you take drugs for medical purposes, carry a letter of authority from your doctor.

Duty-free allowances

The duty-free allowances are 1 litre of spirits, 200 cigarettes or 225gm of tobacco, and 25ml of perfume.

Driving

(*Also refer to Public Transport, especially Car Hire on p186.*)

Driving is on the left in Tanzania, the same as in many other former British colonies.

However, at times you will find the locals driving wherever they can, so beware! To drive in Tanzania you will need to be between 25 and 70, to have two years' minimum experience and to bring your national driving licence. In Zanzibar, you will need an International Driving Permit. If you are in transit from another country a *Carnet de Passage* saves much hassle. Check with your national driving association.

The standards of driving are often atrocious compared with Europe or America. So drive defensively, assuming other drivers will behave erratically. Look out for potholes, animals, people and speed bumps. Beware of buses; they are almost always driven far too fast and very aggressively. Check your spares before you set off. Take two spare tyres. If you break down, follow the normal African custom of scattering branches and foliage (whatever is available) in front and behind your vehicle as a warning.

If you are not experienced at driving in Africa, seriously consider hiring a

Private fire-fighting company

vehicle with a driver. Generally it will be a lot more pleasurable, and you will have much more opportunity to see things.

Electricity

Tanzania officially has a 220–240 volt system, though in reality voltages vary and power surges are common. The system uses British-style three-pin square plugs.

If you have any sensitive electronic equipment with you, make sure you bring a surge protector.

Though hotels and lodges will have their own generator (and may be totally independent of the 'mains'), power cuts are common, especially at the end of the long dry season, when water for hydroelectricity is running low.

Embassies and high commissions

You will generally only need to contact your embassy in a crisis, such as some serious 'trouble', or if you lose your passport. Often your tour guide will help you first. Although your problem may be deadly serious to you, it may be quite a common problem. It will help, for example, in replacing your lost or stolen passport if you have copies of important documents with you, or are accessible to someone at home, who can then fax them. Contact details for the British High Commission and some of the embassies follow.

UK High Commission
Tel: (022) 211 2953/7159.
Republic of Ireland
Tel: (022) 266 6211.

Lutheran church, Dar es Salaam

USA
Tel: (022) 211 8481/2.
Canada High Commission
Tel: (022) 211 2831.

Emergencies

The emergency telephone number in Tanzania is *112*. However, do not expect the immediate response that is normal in North America or Europe. It may also be that there is no ambulance service that can respond to your call.

Air Ambulance numbers from Tanzania are: *(005) 233 6886; (005) 260 2462; (005) 250 1280.*

In some situations you may need to contact your embassy or high commission.

Health
Inoculations

If you arrive by air, except from a few countries (check which ones), you technically do not require inoculation certificates. Arriving overland, you may

One of Arusha's many coffee shops

be required to have a yellow fever certificate.

However, in practice, it is normally advised that you have the following inoculations and that boosters are up to date: yellow fever; tetanus; polio; typhoid; hepatitis A.

Bilharzia

Bilharzia is a peculiarly tropical condition caused by a parasite, which accesses its host in stagnant or slow-moving water. Swimming pools and the sea are fine, but as a general rule never make contact with fresh water in lakes, pools or rivers unless you are clearly told it is bilharzia-free.

Cholera

Cholera may be present in areas near to where you are staying, but with modern sanitation, it is most unlikely you will be affected.

Dehydration

Dehydration may be a problem, either on its own or as a consequence of another illness. Drink plenty of bottled water, which is readily available everywhere. Make very sure that babies and young children do not become dehydrated, especially if they have 'tummy problems'.

HIV/AIDS

Though Tanzania does not have a problem quite as extreme as some African countries, AIDS is still a major killer. More than 10 per cent of the population are probably infected. Careless sexual behaviour may be deadly dangerous.

Hospitals and clinics

There are hospitals and clinics of varying standards throughout the country. For some conditions, for example parasitic ailments and malaria, treatment in Tanzania may be better than in your home country, such is the specific expertise. There are some good hospitals and clinics where you will receive excellent care if necessary.

Aga Khan is generally regarded as the best hospital.

Ocean Dr, Dar es Salaam,
Tel: (022) 211 4096/5151.

The top clinic, which also includes excellent dental care, is the **Nordic Clinic**.

Valhalla Estate. Tel: (022) 260 1650 or (0741) 325 569. (24 hours.)

Malaria

Do take it seriously. Malaria is still a major killer in Africa, and is caused by being bitten by the anopheles mosquito, which is common in some areas, especially near to water. In addition to taking anti-malaria pills (called prophylactics), avoiding being bitten is the most useful thing you can do. Keep covered up in the evening, especially legs and ankles, use your mosquito net and have insecticide available in your room. Anthisan is very effective for treating the bites of mosquitoes and other insects.

If, on returning home after your visit, you start getting severe flu-like symptoms (fever, headache, aching joints), inform your doctor where you have been travelling. Malaria is generally treatable, but it can be very serious when not treated.

Stomach upsets

Generally, normal standards of hygiene in hotels and safari lodges are superb, but unfortunately stomach upsets come with the territory; even Africans going to the UK or USA get them. When you suffer from an upset, the best advice is to treat it with oral rehydration therapy (sugar and salt solutions) and by drinking plenty of liquids. Some situations will make it necessary to take Imodium-type cures, but this should not be your first response, convenient though it may seem.

Sunburn

Sunburn is a serious problem for many holidaymakers, and skin cancers are increasingly common. Remember you are almost on the equator and even hazy sun will burn. Also, when you are high up, which you will be in much of inland Tanzania, the sun's

Bicycle Africa-style

Language

Swahili is the official language of Tanzania. Although most people you meet will speak some English, they will greatly appreciate it if you learn and speak a little of their language. It will be enjoyable for you too.

Some useful words and phrases

English	Swahili	English	Swahili
Hello	*Jambo*	Hello, peace	*Salaam alekum*
Goodbye	*Kwaheri (pl. Kwaherini)*	How are you?	*Habari?*
Fine, good	*Mzuri*	Please	*Tafadhali (hardly used)*
Thank you	*Asante*	Thank you very much	*Asante sana*
Yes	*Ndio*	No	*Hapana*
Father	*Baba*	Mother	*Mama*
Child	*Mtoto*	Older man	*Mzee (to show respect)*
Today	*Leo*	Tomorrow	*Kesho*
Slowly	*Pole pole*	Quickly	*Haraka*
Welcome	*Karibu (pl. Karibuni)*	May I come in?	*Hodi?*
Where is it?	*Iko wapi?*	How was the trip?	*Habari ya safari?*

Days of the week

English	Swahili	English	Swahili
Monday	*Jumatatu*	Tuesday	*Jumane*
Wednesday	*Jumatano*	Thursday	*Alhamisi*
Friday	*Ijumaa*	Saturday	*Jumamosi*
Sunday	*Jumapili*		

Numbers

English	Swahili	English	Swahili
One	*Moja*	Two	*Mbili*
Three	*Tatu*	Four	*Ine*
Five	*Tano*	Six	*Sita*
Seven	*Saba*	Eight	*Nane*
Nine	*Tisa*	Ten	*Kumi*

rays will be more intense as the atmosphere thins out.

Use high-factor sun block, and wear a hat when out in the sun. Protect arms hanging out of vehicles.

Tsetse flies

Tsetse fly bites can be a problem in some bush-savannah areas. Best ensure you will be travelling in a vehicle which can be totally enclosed.

Insurance

Adequate travel insurance is absolutely essential when travelling to African countries, but first check your domestic insurance; you may already be covered. If you are making several trips a year, it is much cheaper to take out annual insurance.

Ensure you have sufficient coverage. Do you have enough cover for single, expensive items like cameras and laptops? If you do have to make a claim, make sure you retain all the receipts.

Internet and email

Africa has taken to the internet just like the rest of the world, and there are many internet cafés in Dar es Salaam and other towns. Many hotels have internet access, some in every room.

Maps

Maps are improving. In general, both for the whole country and for national parks, the maps produced by Harms IC Verlag are the best. The maps available are:

- Tanzania, Rwanda and Burundi 1:400,000
- Zanzibar and Pemba 1:100,000
- Most major national parks

In addition there are pictorial maps of some tourist areas by Giovanni Tombazzi.

Jacana Media are also starting to produce high-quality maps of some wildlife areas, and these publications contain a wealth of eco-information. The first titles are Ngorongoro and Serengeti.

Major map sellers are: UK: Stanfords *www.stanfords.co.uk*; USA: Rand McNally *www.randmcnally.com*; Australia: Mapland *www.mapland.co.au*

Media

Tanzania has a small range of daily and weekly newspapers, written in both English and Swahili. The *Daily News* is the number one, and oldest, daily. Being government owned it grinds out a predictable line on most stories. Others are published by IPP, who produce the daily *Guardian*, and *The East African*, which provides weekly coverage of Tanzania, Kenya and Uganda. *Travel News*, a monthly from Nairobi, deals with new developments in tourism and can be useful to the independent traveller.

As well as the now ubiquitous satellite channels, free-to-view TV includes Agape TV, EATV, ITV, Star TV and TVT. BBC World Service radio is also available on FM locally.

Watertaxi

Useful contacts
Tourism Confederation of Tanzania.
Tel: (255) 22 213 6177.
www.tanzaniatourismonline.com
Hotel Association of Tanzania (HAT).
Tel: (255) 22 212 5022.
hatezsecretary@gmail.com
**Tanzania Association of Tour
Operators (TATO).**
Tel: (255) 27 250 4188.
www.tatotz.org
**Tanzania National Parks Authority
(TANAPA).**
Tel: (255) 27 250 3471.
www.tanzaniaparks.com
**Ngorongoro Conservation Area
Authority (NCAA).**
Tel: (255) 27 253 7019.
www.ngorongoro-crater-africa.org

Money matters
Although other currencies may be
accepted, prices will usually be in
Tanzania shillings.

Visa and American Express cards are
widely accepted, though be prepared
for a 5 per cent mark-up for credit

cards. Other credit cards such as
Diners Club and MasterCard are
not so useful.

Automated teller machines (ATMs)
are widely available, especially in main
towns, and they take the usual cards.
However, as with much electronic
technology, it is not as reliable in
Tanzania as you may be used to back
home, especially the backup phone
systems. So avoid relying on ATMs as
your source of cash.

Exchanging money
The best advice is to use foreign
exchange offices called Forex. Their
rates are usually the best, their service is
quick and they are everywhere. Banks
often have poorer rates and are
notoriously slow.

Never change money on the street.
You are bound to lose out in one way
or another.

Traveller's cheques
These are accepted, but both your
passport and proof of purchase are

often required. In some banks it is also very time-consuming.

Hotels

They will change money, but rates are often extremely poor.

Opening hours

Most shops are open from 8.30am–12.30pm & 2–5pm, although some shops stay open until 7pm. They are also open on Saturday mornings.

Railway station, Dar es Salaam

Government offices are open from 8am–3pm.

Banks are open 8.30am–4pm and on Saturdays until 1pm.

Dukas (the small convenience stores and kiosks) are open all hours.

Police

Dealing with the police can often be a delicate area. Most of your contact with police will be at road checkpoints, usually strips of rusty spikes across the road.

Stop when asked, be polite and use normal greetings. Even offer to shake hands. It may be that you are being stopped for a good reason, but it is just as likely that you are expected to pay a bribe or a fine for some simple trumped-up charge. Any pretence can be used. In most cases, tourists are not a target for corrupt police, but it is not uncommon, and you may have to decide whether to pay an on-the-spot fine of Tsh20,000 or try to bargain your way out of it. Throughout Africa, with police pay almost always low, such a situation is sadly inevitable.

TANZANITE

Tanzanite is a beautiful blue or violet gemstone, only 'discovered' in 1967. It is mined mainly in the Meerani Hills between Moshi and Arusha, and comes out of the ground a brownish colour. However, when heated to over 400ºC (752ºF), it takes on a range of lovely blue shades. The stones are then cut in the normal way to produce faceted gemstones.

Mining is generally poorly run, with a series of awful disasters in recent years, with great loss of life.

The stones cost from $100–$500 per carat, depending on their quality. Buy only from reputable sources. Stones should come with an authentication certificate from the Tanzanite Laboratory.

Post offices

Most places have post offices and things do seem to work, albeit a bit slower than in Europe or North America.

Opening hours are generally 8am–4.30pm weekdays and on Saturday mornings.

Tanzanite jewellery

Poste Restante is available, though it is often slow and there is a small fee.

When posting mail, generally allow about 5 days to Europe and 10 days to the USA. On the whole, mail is reliable.

Your hotel or lodge will also usually receive mail for posting.

The usual couriers are also present in Tanzania, for example FedEx, DHL, UPS etc., and their rates are just as frightening as at home!

Public transport

Most readers will probably have transport already arranged as part of their holiday. However, using public transport is one way of meeting local folk, and you may wish to try it occasionally.

Buses

Most Tanzanians travel by bus. Generally buses are crowded and uncomfortable. However, you do get to meet the locals! One other issue which you may wish to consider is that buses, and road transport in general, have a dreadful safety record, largely due to speeding. Each year there are horrendous accidents involving buses.

Trains

Tanzania has two railway lines, which presently function for passengers – the TAZARA line from Dar es Salaam to Zambia, and the line from Dar es Salaam to Kigoma (Lake Tanganyika) and Mwanza (Lake Victoria). They offer a leisurely way to see parts of the countryside that are often inaccessible by roads.

Ferries

There are ferries on all the main lakes, and from Dar es Salaam, and some other ports, to Zanzibar and Pemba. Some are high-speed catamarans and are an attractive alternative to flying. There are several companies operating from the Samora Road ferry terminal in Dar es Salaam.

Planes

There are air services to all parts of the country from Dar es Salaam International Airport, which is about 15km (9 miles) southwest of the city. The fact that it takes three hours to fly to Mwanza or Kigoma is an indication of the size of the country.

Car hire

Car hire is available in almost all towns. However, it is expensive in comparison with most other tourist destinations. It is often normal for the car to come with a driver. Also you will need to consider whether you will need a 4-wheel-drive vehicle. This will depend on the season and the state of the roads. For a visit to a national park, you must have a 4×4, preferably a Land Cruiser or Land Rover. As usual, carefully check what your liabilities as hirer are.

Snakes

Many people imagine that in the tropics there will be snakes everywhere. However, even in areas with lots of snakes, you are most unlikely to see one, and even less likely to be bitten. For most travellers it is not an issue, though anyone bitten must be treated quickly and correctly.

Sustainable tourism

Thomas Cook is a strong advocate of ethical and fairly traded tourism and believes that the travel experience should be as good for the places visited as it is for the people who visit them. That's why we firmly support The Travel Foundation, a charity that develops solutions to help improve and protect holiday destinations, their environment, traditions and culture.

Practical guide

CONVERSION TABLE

FROM	TO	MULTIPLY BY
Inches	Centimetres	2.54
Feet	Metres	0.3048
Yards	Metres	0.9144
Miles	Kilometres	1.6090
Acres	Hectares	0.4047
Gallons	Litres	4.5460
Ounces	Grams	28.35
Pounds	Grams	453.6
Pounds	Kilograms	0.4536
Tons	Tonnes	1.0160

To convert back, for example from centimetres to inches, divide by the number in the third column.

MEN'S SUITS

Tanzania/UK	36	38	40	42	44	46	48
Rest of Europe	46	48	50	52	54	56	58
USA	36	38	40	42	44	46	48

DRESS SIZES

Tanzania/UK	8	10	12	14	16	18
France	36	38	40	42	44	46
Italy	38	40	42	44	46	48
Rest of Europe	34	36	38	40	42	44
USA	6	8	10	12	14	16

MEN'S SHIRTS

Tanzania/UK	14	14.5	15	15.5	16	16.5	17
Rest of Europe	36	37	38	39/40	41	42	43
USA	14	14.5	15	15.5	16	16.5	17

MEN'S SHOES

Tanzania/UK	7	7.5	8.5	9.5	10.5	11
Rest of Europe	41	42	43	44	45	46
USA	8	8.5	9.5	10.5	11.5	12

WOMEN'S SHOES

Tanzania/UK	4.5	5	5.5	6	6.5	7
Rest of Europe		38	38	39	39	40	41
USA		6	6.5	7	7.5	8	8.5

To find out what you can do to make a positive difference to the places you travel to and the people who live there, please visit *www.thetravelfoundation.org.uk*

Telephones

Telephones can be erratic and frustratingly unreliable. However, in theory, most places now have automatic dialling, and there are TTC (Tanzania Telecom) offices in all main towns, from which you can dial abroad. If you are desperate to keep in touch, you may well buy a mobile phone, or a new simcard if your phone is compatible.

Tembo – typical of Zanzibar's helpful taxi drivers

Most tourist locations now have cellphone coverage.

Outside TTC offices there are cardphones where you can use prepaid telephone cards (*kadi ya simu*). Also there is a growing number of private telephone bureaux. Hotels will almost always have fax facilities, which are usually available to guests.

Time

Tanzania time is three hours ahead of GMT. If you come from a country with 'daylight saving' in the summer, for example the UK, the difference will vary accordingly.

The hours of daylight and darkness are roughly equal, and so Swahili refers to the 12 hours of the day and the 12 hours of the night. For instance, 7am is called *saa moja*, 'one o'clock' or the first hour of the day; 7pm is *saa moja usiku*, first hour in the evening.

Depending on how far east or west you are, sunrise is between 6am and 7am, with sunset between 6pm and 7pm. Many people are surprised how quickly it becomes dark in the tropics, once the sun goes down.

Tipping

This is a slightly difficult area, because it is quite easy for visitors to totally 'rock the boat' in either direction. One starts from the realisation that what a Tanzanian worker earns in a month, you will earn in a morning. Therefore it is normal to tip. Depending on the service, a normal small tip will be

Tsh200 up to perhaps Tsh1,000. However, if you are on safari, with a 'driver-guide' it will be considered normal for everyone in the vehicle to give the driver a substantial tip of perhaps £5–£10 ($8–$15), depending on your satisfaction with the safari. Such a tip is considered to be part of the driver's normal wage.

Toilets

Some toilets, especially in hotels and good restaurants, are excellent and well up to international standards. On the other hand, some will be the worst experiences of your holiday, not to say your life! Most public toilets are simply awful. Generally assume in these circumstances that you bring your own toilet paper. Be prepared, on safari, to 'go' in the bush.

Tourist information

Guide books worth looking at include the *Insight Guide: Tanzania and Zanzibar*, which is well written and beautifully illustrated. The *Rough Guide to Tanzania* has minimal photography apart from animals, but it is full of interesting detail. Double-check on important detail with the nearest high commission or embassy. Visa requirements are misquoted in at least one Tanzania book published recently. Next, check out the **Tanzania Tourist Corporation.**
Tel: (022) 213 1555, fax: (022) 211 6420.
info@tanzaniaodyssey.com
www.tanzaniaodyssey.com

Zanzibar Commission for Tourism
Tel: (024) 223 3485/6,
fax: (024) 223 3448.
Amaan Rd.
PO Box 1410, Zanzibar.
zanzibartourism@zanzibartourism.net
www.zanzibartourism.net

Travellers with disabilities

Tanzania is not the easiest country in which to travel if you are in a wheelchair. Though the people are very friendly and helpful, many of the situations in which you might find yourself are not.

There is almost no provision for wheelchairs on pavements and in many public buildings. The ramps, which are a normal expectation in the West, are non-existent.

Some hotels and safari lodges are wheelchair-friendly, but many are not, even when they claim to be. Generally, Tanzanian taxis are too small for wheelchairs, as are the entrances to most buses and also the corridors on trains.

However, on the brighter side, the luxury buses, which run between main towns and between Arusha and Kenya, have enough room for wheelchairs. Also most safari vehicles not only have adequate space, but also are usually very well sprung, making for a comfortable ride.

The following websites offer advice.
www.holidaycare.org.uk (UK)
www.access-able.com (USA)

Index

Acknowledgements

Thomas Cook Publishing wishes to thank the following photographers, libraries and associations for their assistance in the preparation of this book, to whom the copyright belongs.

Photographs are by DAVID AND ROSEMARY WATSON except as follows:
FOX SAFARIS 163, 165a
FUNDU LAGOON 122, 124, 125 and 157
JOANNE KREIG 181
JON HILL 56, 75, 92, 94a, 94b, 95, 97 and 99
MARLBOROUGH SCHOOL 80
RUBONDO ISLAND CAMP 8, 88b, 89, 90a, 90b, 91, 165b and 166a
SERENA HOTELS 45, 134, 151, 160b, 168 and 169b
WIKIMEDIA COMMONS 119 (Martin Zeise), 130 (Matthias Krämer)
WORLD PICTURES 108, 179

Proofreader: IAN FAULKNER for CAMBRIDGE PUBLISHING MANAGEMENT LTD

SEND YOUR THOUGHTS TO
BOOKS@THOMASCOOK.COM

We're committed to providing the very best up-to-date information in our travel guides and constantly strive to make them as useful as they can be. You can help us to improve future editions by letting us have your feedback. If you've made a wonderful discovery on your travels that we don't already feature, if you'd like to inform us about recent changes to anything that we do include, or if you simply want to let us know your thoughts about this guidebook and how we can make it even better – we'd love to hear from you.

Send us ideas, discoveries and recommendations today and then look out for your valuable input in the next edition of this title. And, as an extra 'thank you' from Thomas Cook Publishing, you'll be automatically entered into our exciting prize draw.

Emails to the above address, or letters to Travellers Project Editor, Thomas Cook Publishing, PO Box 227, Coningsby Road, Peterborough PE3 8SB, UK.

Please don't forget to let us know which title your feedback refers to!